The Compassion
Storybook
BIBLE

By Crystal Bowman and Sue Schlesman

End Game Press books may be purchased in bulk at special discounts for sales promotion, corporate gifts, ministry, fund-raising, or educational purposes. Special editions can also be created to specifications. For details, contact Special Sales Dept., End Game Press, P.O. Box 206, Nesbit, MS 38651 or info@endgamepress.com. Visit our website at www.endgamepress.com.

Library of Congress Control Number: 2024936891
Hardcover ISBN: 9781637971246
eBook ISBN: 9781637972311

Images from DianaDesignLab, Design Candy Studio Art, Lyrical Designs, Adobe Stock and Deposit Photo
Interior Design by TLC Book Design, *TLCBookDesign.com*

Published in association with Karen Neumair of the Credo Communications, LLC

Printed in the United States of America
10 9 8 7 6 5 4 3 2 1

Dedicated to our grandchildren, and the ones yet to be born—
We pray that you will seek Jesus with all your hearts,
that you will be filled with God's grace and compassion,
and that you will love others the way He loves you.

—Crystal and Sue

How to Use This Bible

You are holding a unique kind of children's Bible. Rather than telling superhero Bible stories, this Bible tells simple stories of ordinary, flawed people like us—people who experienced extraordinary compassion and forgiveness from God. Every story conveys God's love for people and shows us all how we can love one another. We believe when your children understand God's compassion, they will grow in compassion toward one another.

Every chapter of *The Compassion Storybook Bible* tells a Bible story and references its location in the Holy Bible. Every story is followed by a focus verse and three discussion questions (one comprehension, one inference, and one application). A sample prayer is included, which incorporates the theme and application of the story. The table of contents tells you which Bible character is highlighted in each story. We pray the combination of these features will give you a framework for heart-changing conversations with the children in your life.

We are overwhelmed by God's empathy and compassion for us. He loves us, regardless of who we are, where we come from, or what we've done. This Bible storybook shows this has always been God's way.

Blessings,
Crystal Bowman and Sue Schlesman

Table of Contents

And what does the Lord require of you? To act justly and to love mercy and to walk humbly with your God.

MICAH 6:8, NIV

A World for Love

Genesis 1-2

DID YOU KNOW GOD made our big, beautiful world because He loves you? Even before you were born, God was thinking about you and creating a world where you could live. Everything you would see, smell, feel, hear, and taste was made to remind you about how much God loves you.

Before time ever began, God spoke into the darkness and made light. He divided the light and dark into day and night. He created

earth and sky, land and water, mountains, deserts, trees, flowers, and grass. He created the sun, moon, and stars to shine from the sky. He created the planets in outer space to orbit the sun. He filled the seas with colorful fish and sea creatures of every size—from mighty sharks and whales to tiny minnows and snails.

Then God made animals on the land—giant elephants, furry koala bears, squirrels with bushy tails, and ladybugs with polka dots. Every animal was special and different from every other animal. God designed seasons like summer, winter, spring, and fall. All of God's creation worked together perfectly. Everything had what it needed to live and grow and multiply.

But God wasn't finished yet. After He created plants, animals, space, sky, water, and land, He made a man and a woman in His image. The man and woman felt emotions like love, anger, happiness, and sadness, just like God did. God's creation took six

days, and after every day, God saw it was good. On the seventh day, God looked at everything He had made, and He saw it was *very* good. Then God rested.

God called the man "Adam" and the woman "Eve." He gave them a beautiful garden to take care of and enjoy. God took walks with Adam and Eve every evening because He loved being with the people He had made, in the world He had made for them.

Everything God made shows He loves us.

Focus Verse

Then God looked over all He had made,
and He saw that it was very good!

GENESIS 1:31, NLT

Talk About It

» How does creation show that God loves us?

» What is your favorite thing in nature that
God made?

» What is one way you can care for God's
creation?

LET'S PRAY

DEAR GOD, thank You for creating our
beautiful world and for creating me in
Your image. Amen.

The First Sin

Genesis 3

GOD LOVED ADAM AND EVE, so He gave them the choice to trust Him or not to trust Him. One day, Eve stood in the Garden of Eden, looking at a beautiful tree called the "Tree of Knowledge of Good and Evil." It was the only tree God told Adam and Eve they couldn't eat from.

Now Satan was an angel who had disobeyed God. God had to kick him out of heaven. Satan wanted to destroy God's plan for creation. So Satan made himself look like a snake and talked to Eve in the garden.

He tricked Eve into thinking God was unfair. Satan lied and said, "Did God really say you couldn't eat from any tree in the garden?"

"No," she answered. "We can eat from any tree except this one. And God said we couldn't touch it, either. If we do, we'll die."

God didn't say they couldn't *touch* it, so that part wasn't true. But sometimes, when people don't understand a rule, they lie about it being harder than it is.

"You won't die," said Satan. "In fact, if you eat the fruit, you will get even smarter than you already are. That's why God doesn't want you to eat it. You'll become just like God. You'll know everything."

Satan's answer was partly a lie. God wasn't jealous or prideful. He only wanted to protect Eve and Adam from the pain of doing wrong.

Eve thought that becoming just like God would be a wonderful thing. So Eve ate the fruit, and Adam ate it, too. Then they realized their pride and disobedience, and they were ashamed. They tried to hide in the bushes so God wouldn't see them. But God called to Adam, "Where are you?"

When God saw Adam and Eve hiding, He made clothes for them out of animal skins. He said they would have to leave the garden and work hard to survive. This was not the plan God wanted for them, but He loved Adam and Eve enough to give them another chance. The world God created was not the same anymore, but God's love for the people He made would never change.

God still loves people even when they mess up.

Focus Verse

But the Lord God called to the man. The Lord said, "Where are you?"

GENESIS 3:9, ICB

Talk About It

» How did Satan trick Eve into thinking God wasn't fair?

» Why should Eve have trusted God?

» When someone wants you to disobey a rule, what should you do?

LET'S PRAY

DEAR GOD, even when I know what's right and wrong, it can be hard to do the right thing. Thank You that You love me and give me second chances. Amen.

Brother Trouble

Genesis 4

ADAM AND EVE were sorry they had eaten from the tree after God told them not to. They missed their walks with God in the garden, and their sin made them feel far away from God. But because God loved Adam and Eve, He made a way for them to be close to Him again. They could make an altar from wood and stone and place an offering to God on the altar. Sometimes the offering could be made of grain. Sometimes it was an animal. This would show God they were sorry for their sins, and He would forgive them.

God gave Adam and Eve something new and wonderful—He gave them children named Cain and Abel. Cain grew up to be a farmer, and Abel became a shepherd. One day, Cain and Abel went to worship God like their parents had taught them. Abel took his best lamb and offered it to God. Cain took some of his fruits and vegetables and placed them on the altar, but they were not his best ones.

God was pleased with Abel's offering, but He did not accept Cain's offering. God could see what was in their hearts. Abel loved God and gave his best offering, but Cain's heart was not right with God. Cain became angry and jealous. He thought God was being unfair. So one day, while he and Abel were out in the field together, Cain hurt Abel, and Abel died.

God punished Cain by sending him away from his family, but God also put a mark on Cain's forehead so everyone would know not to punish him again. God wanted Cain to have another chance to start a new life. God also gave another chance to Adam and Eve to be parents. He gave them a new baby boy named Seth. Later, Adam and Eve had many more sons and daughters.

Disobedience hurts God. God understands it's not possible for people to be perfect, so He shows love and mercy, even when His children do wrong. God's compassion helps everyone feel close to Him again.

God's love and mercy were bigger than Cain's sin.

Focus Verse

Each of you must bring a gift.
It should show how much the Lord
your God has blessed you.

DEUTERONOMY 16:17, ICB

Talk About It

» Why did God accept Abel's offering?

» If you have a brother or sister, do you
ever argue about what's fair? Why?

» How do you feel when you say you're
sorry for doing something wrong?

LET'S PRAY

DEAR GOD, help me to give You my best
and love You with all of my heart. Amen.

Noah's Big Boat

Genesis 6-9

ADAM AND EVE'S FAMILY grew and grew until there were many people living in God's beautiful world. But when God looked at the people, His heart was sad. They had forgotten about Him and were doing bad things. He decided to wash everything away with a flood and start the world over.

Noah was one man who loved God. He had a wife and three sons who were married. God was pleased with Noah's family and wanted to save them from the flood. God told Noah to build a giant boat, so that during the flood, Noah's family and a pair of every kind of animal would survive.

God gave Noah exact measurements to follow. The boat, called an ark, was as long as one and a half football fields! Noah had never seen a boat like this, but he and his family obeyed God and began to build it.

Building the ark took Noah and his sons a hundred years! (People lived a long time back then.) When the big boat was finished, Noah put two of every kind of animal, bird, and insect into the ark. His family also went in. Nobody else wanted to come, so God shut the door.

When they were safe inside, the rain started. It rained hard for forty days and forty nights. The rivers and lakes overflowed, and the oceans rose higher than all the mountains in the world. But God saved Noah and his family. They had to work hard feeding the animals and cleaning the messy stalls.

After forty days and nights, the rain stopped. Noah couldn't see land anywhere. How would he know when it was safe to leave? The ark floated around the world for many months until it bumped into the top of a mountain. Noah's family waited inside the ark for the water to go down. Everyone was getting restless.

Eventually, Noah sent out a dove to see if it could find a place to live. The dove brought back an olive branch, so Noah knew the flood was going down. A week later, Noah sent out the dove again. This time, it didn't return. Noah knew the dove had found a home on dry land. He knew it was safe for them to leave the ark where they had been for 371 days!

Then God painted a beautiful rainbow in the sky and promised He would never send a flood to cover the whole earth again.

God made a way for Noah and his family to be safe.

Focus Verse

The waters will never again become
a flood to destroy all life.

GENESIS 9:15, NIRV

Talk About It

» Why did God decide to start over with the
people and animals?

» Do you think Noah took grown-up animals
or baby animals on the ark? Why?

» Have you ever seen a rainbow? How does a
rainbow remind us that God loves people?

LET'S PRAY

DEAR GOD, thank You for making such a
beautiful world and for giving us life. Amen.

Lot Chooses First

Genesis 12-13

ABRAM WAS A MAN who loved God very much. One day God said, "Leave your country and your father's family. I will show you where to go." Abram listened to God and left his home. He took his wife Sarai, his nephew Lot, lots of helpers, and lots of animals.

After a while, Abram and Lot had so many animals and servants that the land became too crowded. There wasn't enough room for both of their families and all their stuff. There wasn't enough grass and water for the animals. There wasn't enough space for their tents. The sheep and goats and cows bumped into each other, and the men who took care of the animals started arguing.

Abram didn't like all this arguing. He wanted everyone to be happy. He said to Lot, "Our people should not argue with each other. The whole land is ahead of us. We are like brothers. We can separate, so we all have enough land."

Abram was a peacemaker. He did something that was very kind and unselfish. He let Lot pick first. He told Lot, "You can choose which way you want to go. If you go to the left, I'll go to the right. If you go right, then I'll go left."

Lot looked over the whole land and saw a place with lots of fresh water and thick, green grass. It looked like a beautiful garden. Lot chose the best land for himself, and Abram went the other way — to the land that was second-best.

Then God spoke to Abram. "Look around you, Abram. Look to the north and south. Look to the east and the west. Someday I will give all this land to your children's children, and to their children too. Get up and walk around, because I am giving you this land."

Even though Lot had the best land for a while, someday God would give Abram's family a much better land that would be their very own.

Being kind and unselfish was more important to Abram than having the best land.

Focus Verse

So Abram said to Lot, "There should be no arguing between you and me. Your herders and mine should not argue either. We are brothers."

GENESIS 13:8, ICB

Talk About It

» Why did Abram and Lot's helpers argue?

» How did Abram solve the problem?

» What can you do when you have a problem with someone in your family?

LORD, help me to be a peacemaker like Abram was. Help me to be unselfish and kind toward others. Amen.

The God Who Sees

Genesis 16, 21

ABRAM AND HIS WIFE SARAI were sad because they didn't have any children, and they were getting old. Sarai had a slave named Hagar, who was from Egypt. Sarai made her work hard. Because Hagar was a slave, she could not quit her job or say "no" to things she didn't want to do, like have a baby for them. But when Sarai found out Hagar was going to have a baby, Sarai was jealous and treated her badly.

Hagar ran away from Sarai into the desert, where the sun burned Hagar's skin, and she couldn't find food or water. Exhausted and alone, Hagar lay down to die. But God saw her and sent an angel to talk to her.

"Don't worry," the angel said to Hagar. "Your son will be the father of a great nation. God understands how hard your life is. Go back to Sarai, and see how God will take care of you."

Hagar thanked God. "You are the God Who sees me," she said.

Even though she was scared, Hagar went back to Sarai. Later, Hagar had a baby boy. She named him Ishmael. Abram loved Hagar's new baby and spent a lot of time playing with him. This made Sarai even more jealous than before, so Sarai sent Hagar and Ishmael back to the desert. Hagar put Ishmael under a bush. Then she sat down and cried.

God heard Hagar crying. He called from heaven, "Do not be afraid. Lift up your son and take his hand. I will make him into a great nation." When Hagar opened her eyes, she saw a well of water and gave her son a drink.

God sent Hagar and Ishmael to a new place where they would be safe to live. God took care of Hagar because she was important to Him. Finally, Hagar was free.

God sees and cares for people who are sad and hurting.

Focus Verse

You are the God who sees me.

GENESIS 16:13, NIRV

Talk About It

» What made Hagar's life so hard and unfair?

» How did God help Hagar when she was being treated badly?

» How can you help someone who is hurting?

LET'S PRAY

DEAR GOD, thank You for taking such good care of me all the time. I love You. Amen.

Stars and Visitors

Genesis 15, 17, 18, 21

ABRAM AND SARAI had been married for many years. They wanted to have children, but God had not given them any. One night, God told Abram to go outside. "Look up into the sky," He said. "Do you see all the stars? There are so many you cannot count them. Your family will be like that."

Abram didn't understand how this could be, but he believed what God told him. God made another promise to Abram, too. He promised that one day He would give Abram's family lots of beautiful land where they could live with their children,

grandchildren, and great-great-great grandchildren. God changed Abram's name to Abraham, and Sarai's name to Sarah. God said, "I will make you the father of many nations and kings will come from you. I will be your God and the God to your children after you."

Abraham and Sarah waited patiently for a son. Eventually, they became too old to have children. They were as old as great-grandparents! They did not understand why God let this happen. Then one day God sent three visitors to Abraham's tent. Abraham ran to meet them. He brought them some water to wash their feet and food to eat. He treated them kindly. He didn't know two of the men were angels and one was the Lord Himself. He also didn't know they had something exciting to tell him!

While they were eating, the Lord said, "I will come back about this time next year, and Sarah will have a son."

Sarah was listening from inside the tent. When she heard the news, she laughed. Sarah knew it was impossible for her to have a baby now, so she thought this was funny. Then the Lord said, "Why did Sarah laugh? Is anything too hard for Me?"

God's promise to Abraham finally came true. Even though they were old, Abraham and Sarah had a baby boy and named him *Isaac*, which means "laughter." Abraham and Sarah were so happy to finally have a child. They learned God always keeps His promises.

God showed kindness to Abraham and Sarah, and they showed kindness to strangers.

"Is anything too hard for the Lord?"

GENESIS 18:14, ICB

Talk About It

» Why were Abraham and Sarah sad?

» Why did Sarah laugh?

» How does God keep His promises to you?

LET'S PRAY

DEAR GOD, when things are hard for me, help me to remember that nothing is impossible for You. Amen.

Twin Brothers

Genesis 25, 27, 32, 33

ABRAHAM'S SON ISAAC married a woman named Rebecca. They had twin boys named Esau and Jacob. Even though they were twins, they were not alike at all! Esau was the oldest twin. He was rugged and hairy. He was a good hunter and liked to be out in the fields. Jacob had smooth skin. He was quiet and liked to stay home to cook with his mother.

One day, Jacob was cooking some stew when Esau came home from hunting. Esau smelled the delicious stew and wanted some right away, because he was hungry. Jacob was not a good brother that day!

He tricked Esau into selling his birthright for a bowl of stew. Everything that belonged to their father, Isaac, would now belong to Jacob, instead of Esau.

When Isaac was very old and could no longer see, Jacob did another bad thing. He put animal hair on his skin so he would smell and feel like Esau when he visited Isaac. Then Jacob asked Isaac to bless him. Isaac gave away the blessing that belonged to Esau.

When Esau found out how Jacob had tricked their father, he was so angry he wanted to kill his brother. Jacob had to run away and live with his uncle in another country for many years. Then one

day, God told Jacob to go back home. By this time Jacob had lots of children, servants, donkeys, sheep, and goats.

As Jacob and his family traveled home, he found out Esau was coming to meet him. Jacob was afraid because he was sure Esau was still angry with him. Jacob sent messengers on ahead, offering gifts and animals to Esau.

When Esau saw Jacob a long way off, he ran to meet him. He threw his arms around his neck and kissed him. Then they both cried. "What are all these animals for?" Esau asked.

"They are gifts for you, so you will accept me," said Jacob.

Esau didn't want the gifts because he already had everything he needed. And he was no longer angry with Jacob for the mean things Jacob had done to him. Esau wanted to help Jacob instead of hurting him.

Even though Jacob mistreated him, Esau was kind to Jacob and loved him as his brother.

Focus Verse

But Esau said, "You don't have to give me gifts, brother. I have enough for myself."

GENESIS 33:9, ERV

Talk About It

» How were Jacob and Esau different?

» Why did Jacob have to leave home?

» What might happen if we are kind to someone who is mean to us?

DEAR GOD, it's hard when someone is mean. Sometimes bad things happen that I don't understand. Help me to love other people even when they are hard to love. Amen.

Joseph Goes to Egypt

Genesis 37-47

JOSEPH WAS ONE of Jacob's sons. He had a baby brother, ten older half-brothers, and a half-sister. You might think nobody paid any attention to Joseph because there were so many children, but the opposite was true. Joseph got all the attention from their father because he was Jacob's favorite son. Jacob made Joseph a colorful coat and taught him at home instead of sending him to work in the fields with his brothers.

Joseph's older half-brothers were jealous and mean to Joseph because of the way their father loved him. They hated Joseph even more when God gave Joseph dreams about becoming the leader of his family. How could he be their leader when he was almost the youngest?

One day, Jacob sent Joseph to check on his brothers while they were watching their father's sheep. The brothers saw Joseph's colorful coat from a distance. "Let's kill him," they said. "Then let's see if his dreams come true." But instead of killing him, they sold him into slavery to some traders passing by. Then they tricked Jacob into thinking Joseph was dead. Jacob cried and cried, and no one could comfort him.

Meanwhile, Joseph was sold in Egypt to a rich man named Potiphar. Joseph worked so hard that Potiphar put him in charge of the whole house. Then Potiphar's wife lied about Joseph, so Potiphar threw Joseph into prison. Joseph was kind and helpful to the jailer and the other prisoners. The head jailor put Joseph in charge of the prisoners.

Years later, Joseph got out of jail because God helped him understand two of the king's dreams. Joseph told the king, named Pharaoh, a plan for saving the country from starving, so Pharaoh put Joseph in charge of the whole country. Joseph was a leader everywhere he went!

Eventually, Joseph's older brothers came to Egypt to buy food. They were afraid when they realized Joseph had the power to put them in prison. Instead of getting back at them, Joseph forgave his brothers for selling him into slavery. He invited them to live in Egypt where he could take care of them. Joseph said, "You intended to harm me, but God intended it all for good." Even though Joseph's brothers were mean to him, they could not stop God's plan to make Joseph a good leader.

Joseph treated his brothers with compassion because he trusted God's plan for his life.

Focus Verse

You intended to harm me,
but God intended it all for good.

GENESIS 50:20, NLT

Talk about It

» Why were Joseph's brothers mean to Joseph?

» Why did Joseph forgive his brothers for selling him into slavery?

» Why do you think some people are mean, even to nice people?

LET'S PRAY

DEAR GOD, help me to forgive people who are not kind to me. I know You will do good things in my life. Amen.

A Brave Sister

Exodus 1-2

A GIRL NAMED MIRIAM crouched in the tall grass along the Nile River in Egypt. She watched for soldiers, boats, hippos, and crocodiles. Her baby brother slept in a basket on the water. She had hidden his basket in the reeds along the river's edge, but now, the basket was floating out into the river!

Miriam was a Hebrew girl. Her people, called the Israelites, lived in Egypt because hundreds of years before, Joseph had brought his family there for safety from a famine. But now the king, called Pharaoh, who was ruling Egypt, didn't remember the story of Joseph saving Egypt from starving. This Pharaoh was afraid that millions of Hebrews would overpower his Egyptian people.

So Pharaoh made the Israelites slaves, who worked hard for the Egyptians and didn't get paid for their work. To make sure their families didn't get any bigger, Pharaoh made a law to kill all the Hebrew baby boys.

As Miriam watched, Pharaoh's daughter, the princess, came to the river to take a bath. She noticed the basket and told one of her helpers to go into the water and get it. When the princess saw the sweet baby and heard him crying, she felt sorry for him. She knew it was dangerous for a baby to float on the river. "This is one of the Hebrew babies," she said. "Someone's hiding him."

Miriam was brave and quickly came out from the weeds to speak to the princess and protect her baby brother. "Shall I find a Hebrew woman to take care of the baby for you?" she asked.

"Yes, please go," said the princess.

Miriam ran to get her mother and brought her back to the river. How amazing would it be for her mother to care for her own child!

"Please take care of this baby, and I will pay you," said the princess. So the baby's mother fed and cared for him until he was old enough to live in the king's palace. Pharaoh's daughter named the boy *Moses*, which means "I drew him out of the water." Moses became her son. Moses was saved!

God helped Miriam to be a brave sister and keep her brother safe.

Focus Verse

When she opened it, Pharaoh's daughter saw the baby. He was crying. She felt sorry for him. "This is one of the Hebrew babies," she said.

EXODUS 2:6, NIRV

Talk About It

» Why didn't Pharaoh want the Israelites to have more children?

» What three people did God use to save Moses?

» Why are God's plans always the best plans?

LET'S PRAY

DEAR GOD, thank You that You are greater than any king or ruler. Help me to always trust Your plans for me and my family. I know You will always protect me. Amen.

A Path to Freedom

Exodus 3-14

THE ISRAELITES LIVED in the land of Egypt for many years. They worked hard and cried out to God for help. Moses had grown up and was living in a place called Midian where he worked as a shepherd.

One day, Moses saw a bush that was on fire. Then he heard God's voice: "I have seen the troubles of My people and heard their cries. I am concerned about their pain and want to deliver them from the Egyptians." God told Moses to go back to Egypt and tell Pharaoh to let the Israelites return to their homeland. Moses was afraid, but God promised Moses that He would help him be the leader Israel needed.

When Moses went to Egypt and told Pharaoh to let the Israelites leave, Pharaoh said, "No way!" Pharaoh wanted to keep the Israelites in his land as slaves. So God sent horrible plagues, one at a time, to the land of Egypt that tormented the Egyptians. But God's love and compassion kept the Israelites safe from all the plagues.

First, the water in the Nile River turned to blood. Then millions of frogs were hopping everywhere, followed by gnats, flies, and sick farm animals. With each plague, Pharaoh said he would let the Israelites leave, but when God took the plagues away, Pharaoh changed his mind.

God sent more plagues like painful boils, pounding hail, swarms of locusts, and days of total darkness. But Pharaoh still said no. Finally, God told the Israelites it was time to leave. He told them to paint their doorposts with blood from a lamb, which would be a sign to keep them safe. Then God sent an angel of death through Egypt. Every house that didn't cover their doorpost with blood watched their firstborn son die. God was showing His people that someday, His Son would die to save them because

God loved them so much. Pharaoh was afraid of God's power, so he let the Israelites leave.

After they were gone, Pharaoh became angry and changed his mind. He sent his army to bring them back. The Israelites walked until they came to the huge Red Sea. They were trapped and could not get across! God told Moses to stretch his staff over the sea. Then God split the deep water down the middle and made a long path for the Israelites to walk through. They escaped to the other side! God saved His people from their hard life in Egypt and promised to always be their God.

God knows when we are hurting, and He wants to help us.

Talk About It

» Why did Pharaoh want to keep the Israelites in Egypt?

» How did God help the Israelites to escape?

» Why does God care about our problems?

LET'S PRAY

DEAR GOD, thank You that You care about me all the time. I know I can tell You about my problems. I know You will hear me and help me. Amen.

Ten Rules of Love

Exodus 20; Deuteronomy 5

FOR MANY WEEKS, the Israelites walked through the wilderness on their way to the land God had promised them. The Israelites had become a big nation with millions of people. God helped them find water when they were thirsty and food when they were hungry. Sometimes, the water poured out of rocks, and sometimes, God made bitter water safe to drink. Every morning, God dropped little bits of bread from heaven called *manna*. In the evening, He sent quail to cover the ground so people could catch them and cook them. Even though the people grumbled and complained, God took care of them because He loved them.

One day, God told Moses to meet with Him on the top of Mount Sinai. Thunder boomed, lightning flashed, and trumpets blared. A thick cloud of smoke covered the mountaintop. The people trembled at the foot of the mountain, while Moses climbed to the top where God was. God gave Moses and the Israelites ten rules to follow called the Ten Commandments. The rules taught the people how to love God and how to love others.

The first four rules are about loving God:

1. You must not have any other god but Me.

2. You must not make an idol or statue to worship.

3. You must not use My name in a way that does not honor Me.

4. You must keep one day special each week, when you worship Me.

The next six rules are about loving other people:

5. Obey your parents. Then you will have a long and full life.

6. Do not kill anyone.

7. Do not take someone's wife or husband away from them.

8. Do not steal.

9. Do not lie.

10. Do not want things that belong to other people.

God said that He would bless the Israelites if they followed His rules. If they didn't follow His rules, they would face many problems. Then God told Moses to tell the people, "You have seen that I talk to you from heaven. Do not make idols from silver or gold or make anything else more important than Me."

God's commandments show us how to love
Him and how to love others.

Focus Verse

I will be very kind to people who love me and obey my commands. I will be kind to their families for thousands of generations.

EXODUS 20:6, ERV

Talk About It

» Why did God want to meet with Moses on Mount Sinai?

» How would the ten rules help the Israelites?

» How can the rules still help us today?

LET'S PRAY

DEAR GOD, thank You for teaching us how to love You and how to love others. Help me to show love to everyone every day. Amen.

Hiding Two Spies

Joshua 2, 5

RAHAB LIVED in a house on the high wall that surrounded the strong city of Jericho. Her window looked out on the beautiful hill country. The people in Jericho didn't know God, but they had heard about God's power, and they knew He protected the Israelites. They knew Moses led God's people through the Red Sea. They heard how God won battles for Israel, gave them food, and kept them safe. They knew that Joshua and the Israelite army had come to conquer them because God wanted to give them back the land of their ancestors Abraham, Isaac, and Jacob.

One day, Rahab heard a knock on her front door. Two men stood there, looking anxious.

"We need a place to hide," they said. "Can we come in?"

Rahab could tell that the men were spies from Israel. They had come to Jericho to learn how to overtake the city. "Come quick!" she said. "I will hide you because I know God is with you."

Rahab took them up to her roof where she was drying flax to make into flour. The spies lay down, and Rahab covered them with blankets and put piles of flax on top of them.

Someone banged at her door. "Open up!" shouted Jericho's soldiers. "We know you're hiding the spies!"

But the soldiers could not find the spies; they did not see them hiding under the flax.

At nighttime, Rahab uncovered the spies. "You are safe to leave, but the city gates are locked to keep your army out. Go hide in the mountains until it's safe. I know your God will help you defeat us. Please show compassion to me and my family when you conquer us. Do not kill us."

"We promise, we won't," said the spies. "Just put a red cord in your window so we know which house is yours. We will protect everyone who's inside. You can join our nation and worship our God with us."

Rahab agreed. She helped the spies escape from Jericho by letting them down a rope from her window. She believed they would keep her promise to save her and her family when they came to take over the city.

Rahab treated the spies with kindness, so the spies promised to do the same.

Focus Verse

Promise me in the name of the Lord
that you will be kind to my family.
I've been kind to you.

JOSHUA 2:12, NIRV

Talk About It

» Where did Rahab live?

» Why did Rahab help the spies?

» How can you show kindness to someone
who is not your friend?

LET'S PRAY

Dear God, thank You for all the ways
that You are kind to me. Please help me
to be kind to others. Amen.

Strong and Brave

Joshua 1-4

JOSHUA BECAME the new leader of the Israelites after Moses died, and God gave him an enormous assignment! God told Joshua, "It's time for you to lead the Israelites across the Jordan River into the land I am giving them." God had promised to give this land to Abraham four hundred years earlier. Now it was time to enter the Promised Land!

Joshua knew he could not lead the Israelites into this new land on his own. But God encouraged Joshua, "Just as I was with Moses, so I will be with you. No one will be able to stop you all your life. I will not leave you. I will never leave you alone."

God gave Joshua special instructions on how to lead the people across the river. Then He said, "Be strong and brave. Be sure to obey all the teachings My servant Moses gave you. If you follow them exactly, you will be successful in everything you do." Two more times God told Joshua, "Be strong and brave."

Since it was harvest season, the Jordan River was overflowing, and the water was deep. As soon as the priests' feet touched the river's edge, the water upstream stopped flowing and piled up in a heap. The Israelites walked across on dry land, just like their mothers and fathers did when they crossed the Red Sea.

Joshua knew their first battle in the Promised Land would be hard. But God sent the Angel of the Lord to let Joshua know God would go with him. The Israelites marched around Jericho exactly the way God had instructed. For six days, they marched around the city one time without saying a word, then went back home. On the seventh day, they marched around the city seven times. Then the priests blasted their trumpets, and Joshua commanded, "Shout! For the Lord has given you the city!"

The walls around Jericho came crashing down, and the Israelites won the battle! Joshua remembered the promise his spies had made to Rahab and sent soldiers to her house to save Rahab and her family. Joshua did exactly what God told him to do, and he remembered God's promise to be with him.

God helped Joshua to be strong and brave for the big job he had to do.

Focus Verse

Remember that I commanded you to
be strong and brave. So don't be afraid.
The Lord your God will be with you
everywhere you go.

JOSHUA 1:9, NLT

Talk About It

» What important job did God give to Joshua?

» What did God say to Joshua three times?

» How can God help you to be brave?

LET'S PRAY

DEAR GOD, I can be strong and brave
because I know You are with me all the
time, just like You were with Joshua. Amen.

New Girl in Town

Ruth 1-4

RUTH GREW UP in a foreign country. She moved to Bethlehem to be with her mother-in-law, Naomi, and take care of her. Ruth felt unimportant and strange in her new town. She was also sad and lonely because her husband had died.

Ruth wanted to start over in this new place, but she and Naomi had nothing to eat and no money to buy food. "I will go into the fields and pick up all the leftover pieces of barley that the farmers drop," said Ruth. "Maybe the scraps will be enough for us to make flour and bread for us to live." Ruth felt embarrassed to pick up the leftovers, but it's what she needed to do to feed herself and Naomi.

Boaz was the owner of the field where Ruth started working. He was a kind and caring man. He noticed how hard Ruth worked, and he gave her lunch. He took her into the shade to cool off and

drink some water. Then he made sure the farmers dropped extra barley, so she would have a lot to take home. He told the farmers they must never make Ruth feel embarrassed for picking up the leftover barley. Boaz invited Ruth to come back every day to work in his field where he could keep her safe.

When Ruth told Naomi who was helping her, Naomi clapped her hands and jumped up and down. Boaz was one of her relatives. The Jewish law said that if someone lost their land and husband, a close relative of the family could marry them, buy back their land, and give it to them as an inheritance.

And that's exactly what Boaz did! Boaz married Ruth, and soon they had a little boy named Obed. Now Naomi and Ruth would be safe forever.

Boaz was humble and compassionate to Ruth because Ruth was humble and compassionate to Naomi. God blessed Ruth for her kindness to Naomi. He gave her a new life and a new family in a new town.

God blesses us when we are kind to others who need our help.

Focus Verse

"Thank God for a girl like you!" [Boaz] exclaimed. "For you are being even kinder to Naomi now than before."

RUTH 3:10, TLB

Talk About It

» What did Ruth do to help Naomi?

» Why did Boaz marry Ruth?

» Do you know any new kids in your church, school, or neighborhood? How can you make them feel safe and happy in a new place?

DEAR GOD, thank You for grownups who love me and take care of me. Amen.

Courage to Help

Esther 1-8

ESTHER WAS AN ORPHAN who lived in Persia. She lived with her cousin Mordecai, who raised her. Many years before, their great-grandparents had been captured and taken out of Israel to live in the country of Persia.

The king of Persia was a selfish man named Xerxes, who divorced his wife for not obeying him. To replace her, Xerxes kidnapped all the young, beautiful women in his empire and kept them in his castle until he was ready to choose a new wife from the group. The women could never leave.

Esther was beautiful and kind, and Xerxes picked her for his new queen. Esther was afraid of what Xerxes would do to her if she didn't make him happy. She didn't understand why God let this happen to her.

Mordecai was also scared for Esther's safety because she was Jewish, not Persian. Mordecai told

Esther to keep this a secret because the Persians did not treat the Jews kindly. Mordecai walked outside the palace walls every day to find out how Esther was doing. She would wave to him from her window or send him messages to say she was okay.

While Mordecai waited for messages, he met Haman, an evil leader who hated the Jews. Haman hatched a plan to kill all the Jews in Persia on a single day! When Mordecai found out Haman's order, he told Esther to ask Xerxes to help them.

But Esther was afraid.

Mordecai told Esther, "If you do not save us, God will send someone else to do it. But who knows if this is the reason you were made queen? What if this is the reason God made you?"

Esther and her servants prayed for three days. Then she went to talk to Xerxes. The king smiled at her. She told him about Haman's plan to get rid of the Jews and asked for his help. Xerxes was angry! He punished Haman and passed a new law so the Jews could protect themselves. Then Xerxes gave Mordecai Haman's job. Now Esther could see Mordecai any time she wanted!

Esther had the courage to speak up when she was afraid. She saved God's special people, and God saved her!

Focus Verse

"You might keep quiet at this time. Then someone else will help.... And who knows, you may have been chosen queen for just such a time as this."

ESTHER 4:14, ICB

Talk About It

» What was Esther afraid of?

» Why did Haman want to kill all the Jews?

» How did Esther get the courage to ask for Xerxes' help?

LET'S PRAY

DEAR GOD, I know You never leave me alone. Help me to listen to Your words when I'm afraid. I know You have a special plan for my life. Amen.

Hearing God Speak

1 Samuel 1-3

HANNAH WANTED to be a mom. Every year that she was married, she hoped for a baby. Every year, she was disappointed. The other mothers made fun of her because they had many children, and she had none.

One year, when it was time to visit the Temple, Hannah went with her husband. She got on her knees to pray. "LORD, You are the ruler over everything. Do You see how sad I am? Don't forget about me! Please give me a son! If You do, I'll give him back to the LORD. Then he will serve the LORD all the days of his life."

God understood Hannah's sadness and answered her prayer. The next year, Hannah had a beautiful baby boy. She named him *Samuel*, which means "God has heard." Hannah loved cuddling her soft, chubby baby and making him smile. Hannah felt grateful to God. She wanted Samuel to serve God for his whole life.

Hannah remembered her promise to God. When Samuel was three years old, she took him to the Temple so he would be in God's house every day

with the high priest, Eli. Every year Hannah brought Samuel a new coat and hugged him tight. She was pleased that her boy loved God, and God was pleased with Hannah's love for Him. God gave her three more sons and two daughters.

Samuel grew up in the Temple and helped Eli. One night, when Samuel was still a young boy, he woke up to hear, "Samuel! Samuel!"

Samuel ran to Eli's bed. "Here I am. What do you need?"

Eli rubbed his eyes and squinted at Samuel in the darkness. "What? I didn't call you. Go back to bed."

This happened two more times before Eli said, "I know what's happening. The Lord is calling to you. The next time God calls you, say, "Speak, Lord. I am listening."

God called Samuel again as He stood by the altar. "Samuel! Samuel!"

This time, Samuel said, "Speak, Lord. I am listening."

Then God told Samuel what He wanted him to do. For all of Samuel's life, God spoke to him and gave him important messages to share with others. Samuel became the greatest prophet that Israel ever had because he listened when God talked to him.

God cared so much about Samuel that He talked to him.

Focus Verse

Samuel said, "Speak, Lord. I am
your servant, and I am listening."

1 SAMUEL 3:10, ICB

Talk About It

» How did God answer Hannah's prayer?

» What did Samuel listen for?

» How does God talk to you? What things
does God want you to do?

DEAR GOD, help me to listen for Your
voice. I want to obey You and always do
what You tell me. Amen.

A Shepherd Praises God

Psalm 145; 1 Samuel 16-17

DAVID WAS the youngest son of Jesse. He had seven older brothers. While David's brothers did important work, David spent his days in the fields watching his father's sheep. While the sheep were sleeping and eating, David sang songs to God and wrote poems about how wonderful and amazing he knew God was.

At night, David stayed with the sheep to protect them from wild animals. When he looked at the huge, dark sky, he saw millions of twinkling stars. David knew only a great God could have made all those stars light up the sky for him. David wondered why God cared so much about him.

David knew God was always with him. Once, when David was watching the sheep, a bear attacked the flock. David quickly pulled out his slingshot and killed the bear with one stone. Another time, a mountain lion attacked, and David again protected his father's sheep. Out in the pasture, David learned to trust God, even when he was all alone.

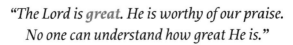

David wrote many songs about God's love and compassion for him. They are called "psalms" in the Bible. In Psalm 145, David wrote words to praise God for all the ways that He is good.

"The Lord is great. He is worthy of our praise. No one can understand how great He is."

*"The Lord is **kind** and shows mercy.
He does not become angry quickly but is full of **love**."*

*"The Lord is **good** to everyone.
He is **merciful** to all He has made."*

*"The Lord will **keep** His promises.
With love He takes **care** of all He has made."*

*"The Lord **helps** those who have been defeated.
He **takes care** of those who are in trouble."*

*"All living things look to You for food.
And You **give** it to them at the right time."*

*"You open Your hand, and You **satisfy** all living things."*

*"The Lord is **close** to everyone who prays to Him."*

*"He **gives** those who fear Him what they want."*

*"He **listens** when they cry, and He **saves** them." (ICB)*

David understood the greatness of God's compassion. Nothing felt better than God's love!

God is loving, merciful, and kind to His creation.

Focus Verse

Everything the Lord does is right. With love He takes care of all He has made.

PSALM 145:17, ICB

Talk About It

» When did David enjoy talking to God?

» Why did David praise God?

» How can you praise God?

LET'S PRAY

DEAR GOD, You are so amazing and wonderful and great. Thank You for loving me so much! Amen.

Kindness from a King

1 Samuel 16; 1 Samuel 18; 2 Samuel 9

KING SAUL was Israel's first king. He did things his own way and didn't listen to God, so God wanted to give Israel a new king. God told Samuel to go to Jesse's home in Bethlehem. "I have chosen one of Jesse's sons to be king," He said.

Samuel met Jesse and his sons. They were so tall and handsome! Samuel was sure God would choose one of them to be the next king. But God told Samuel, "The Lord doesn't see things the way you see them. People judge by outward appearance, but the Lord looks at the heart."

As each brother walked by Samuel, God said, "He is not the one."

Samuel asked Jesse if he had another son. "My son David is in the fields watching the sheep," said Jesse.

"Send for him," Samuel said.

When David arrived, God told Samuel, "This is the one; anoint him." God knew David would be a good king because he loved God with all his heart.

Samuel poured oil on David's head to show God had chosen David to be the next king of Israel. But David didn't become king right away. He waited until the time was right.

David became good friends with King Saul's son Jonathan. They promised they would love God and protect each other's families. They promised to be best friends forever.

Many years later when David became king, he asked one of Saul's servants, "Is anyone still alive from Saul's family?"

The servant said, "Jonathan's son Mephibosheth is still alive, but he cannot walk."

David knew Mephibosheth would not own any land or be able to take care of himself. In Bible times, most people who couldn't walk sat on the ground and begged for food. "Bring Mephibosheth to me," said David.

When Mephibosheth arrived, he quivered with fear and bowed to the ground. "Don't be afraid!" said King David. "I want be kind to you because of my promise to your father, Jonathan. I will give you the land that belonged to your grandfather, Saul, and you may live with me at the palace."

From that day on, Mephibosheth ate at the king's table. David treated him like a son.

David's compassion for Mephibosheth showed what was in David's heart.

Focus Verse

The king then asked him, "Is anyone still alive from Saul's family? If so, I want to show God's kindness to them."

2 SAMUEL 9:3, NLT

Talk About It

» How do you think Mephibosheth felt when David told him to live at the palace?

» How did David's kindness change Mephibosheth's life?

» What can you do to be kind to someone today?

DEAR GOD, please fill my heart with love and compassion, so I will treat others with kindness. Amen.

LET'S PRAY

Wise Words

1 Kings 3; Proverbs 3-21

Solomon became the king of Israel after his father, David, died. Solomon loved God and obeyed Him. One night God came to Solomon in a dream and said, "Ask for anything you want, and I will give it to you."

Solomon answered God. "You were kind to my father, David, and now, You are being kind to me by making me king. Please give me wisdom, so I can rule Your people in the right way. Help me to know the difference between right and wrong by making me wise."

Solomon could have asked for money. He could have asked God to make him famous. He could have asked for a long life. But the most important thing to him was being a good ruler, so he could be kind and fair to God's people. God was pleased with Solomon's answer. He gave Solomon a wise and understanding heart. God also gave Solomon the things he didn't ask for, because He knew Solomon's heart was right. God told Solomon, "During your life no other king will be as great as you. Follow Me, and obey My laws and commands. Do this as your father David did. If you do, I will also give you a long life."

Besides being the king of Israel, Solomon wrote some books in the Bible. The book of Proverbs has many of his wise sayings. He wrote them to help people do what is right, just, and fair. These are some of the proverbs of Solomon:

Whenever you are able, do good to people who need help.
PROVERBS 3:27 (ICB)

Kind words are like honey—
sweet to the soul and healthy for the body.
PROVERBS 16:24 (NLT)

A friend loves you all the time.
brother is always there to help you.
PROVERBS 17:17 (ICB)

*Being kind to the poor is like lending to the Lord. The
Lord will reward you for what you have done.*
PROVERBS 19:17 (ICB)

*The Lord is more pleased when we do what is right and
just than when we offer Him sacrifices.*
PROVERBS 21:3 (NLT)

Solomon understood the importance of treating
others with kindness. God gave him what he asked
for because he wanted to be a good king.

Solomon knew that being kind was more
important than being rich and famous.

Focus Verse

Give me an understanding heart so that I can govern Your people well and know the difference between right and wrong.

1 KINGS 3:9, NLT

Talk About It

» What did God say to Solomon?

» How did Solomon answer Him?

» Why is it important to have wisdom and how can we get it?

LET'S PRAY

DEAR GOD, thank You that You will give me wisdom if I ask. Help me to be wise in the way I treat others. Amen.

A Promise of Care

1 Kings 17

ELIJAH THE PROPHET of God stood before King Ahab and gave him a message. "God will keep it from raining for the next three years because you have turned Israel away from worshiping God."

Then God told Elijah, "Go and hide. I will take care of you and keep you safe."

Elijah traveled to a valley where he drank water from a creek. God sent ravens every day with meat and bread for Elijah to eat. The ravens let Elijah take the food from their mouths without biting him.

Eventually, the creek dried up, so God told Elijah, "Go to a village called Zarephath. A widow will take care of you there."

Elijah obeyed God and went to Zarephath. When he got there, he saw a woman picking up sticks for a fire. "Can you make dinner for me?" he asked.

The widow looked sad and hungry. "My husband died. I only have enough oil and flour to make one loaf of bread for myself and my son. Then we will die too."

"Don't be afraid," said Elijah. "Make some bread for me. God promises that your oil and flour will never run out."

The widow obeyed Elijah's words because she knew they came from God. After she made one loaf, she made another and another. Every time she poured out the oil and flour, more oil and flour appeared in the jars! It was a miracle!

After a while, the woman's son got sick and died. "Why is this happening?" she cried. "I have helped you!"

"Don't be afraid. Give me your son," said Elijah.

He carried the boy upstairs and laid him on the bed. He saw the boy's brown eyelashes against his pale cheeks. He remembered the faithfulness of the mother. He heard her sobbing downstairs.

"Oh, God," cried Elijah, "let this boy's life return!" He lay across the boy's chest and prayed.

Suddenly, he felt the boy's chest moving up and down. Breath puffed out of the boy's nose. His eyelids fluttered open, and big brown eyes blinked at Elijah.

Elijah picked up the boy and ran downstairs. "Look! He's alive!"

The woman hugged her son and wouldn't let go of him. "Now I know that God's words are true!" She and Elijah realized God had kept His promise to care for them.

God cared for Elijah and the widow because He loved them.

Focus Verse

I know that the message you have brought from the LORD is true.

1 KINGS 17:24, NIRV

Talk About It

» Why was it hard for Elijah and the widow to get food?

» How did God take care of Elijah and the widow?

» What can you do when you're afraid or you need something?

LET'S PRAY

DEAR GOD, thank You for always taking care of me. Help me to obey You and trust the things You tell me in the Bible. Amen.

A Friendly Lady

2 Kings 4

ELISHA WAS GOD'S prophet to Israel after Elijah died. He traveled across Israel and other countries helping people. One day, as he passed through the town of Shunem, a wealthy woman came out of her house. "Elisha," she said. "I know you are God's prophet. Please come and stay with us whenever you are passing through town."

The woman built a special bedroom for Elisha. She and her husband provided nice meals and loved Elisha's company. Elisha wanted to do something kind for her, but she seemed to have everything she needed. She had a big house, many servants, and a nice husband. She even had a big farm to supply all the food she needed. But the Shunamite woman had no children to love. Her husband had no son to help him on the farm.

Elisha smiled. "By this time next year, you will have a son."

The woman looked worried. "Don't disappoint me," she said.

Elisha's words came true. By the next year, the couple had a beautiful baby boy. They enjoyed playing with him and laughing with him. When he got big enough, he helped his dad in the fields.

One day, the boy got a terrible headache. A servant carried him home, and his mother rocked him in her lap. Then the boy died. His mother carried him to Elisha's room and closed the door. She saddled a donkey and told a servant to ride fast ahead of her, all the way to Mount Carmel where

Elisha was. She didn't tell anyone her son was dead.

When she got to Mount Carmel, she bowed at Elisha's feet, crying. "Didn't I tell you not to disappoint me? I didn't ask you for a son. How could you do this to me?"

Elisha tried to comfort her. "Go home. I'll send my servant."

The woman shook her head. "I'm not leaving until you come with me." She knew God's power rested on Elisha.

Elisha and the woman rode back to her house. Elisha locked himself in his room with the boy. He lay across the boy and prayed. He breathed on him. The boy began to grow warm. Then he sneezed and opened his eyes.

Elisha called the boy's mother. She ran in, fell at Elisha's feet, and worshiped God.

God showed compassion to a kind woman by giving her what she wanted most.

Focus Verse

"About this time next year," Elisha said,
"you will hold a son in your arms."

2 KINGS 4:16, NIV

Talk About It

» How did the Shunamite woman take care of
Elisha?

» Why did the woman ride a long way to get
Elisha?

» What is something important that you pray
to God about?

DEAR GOD, when I am worried about
something, please help me to trust You
with it. I want You to be the Person in
charge of my life. Amen.

A Big Prayer and a Shadow

2 Kings 18, 20

KING HEZEKIAH was twenty-five years old when he began to rule over Judah. He loved God and obeyed the commandments God had given to Moses. He did what was right, just like King David had done. God helped Hezekiah to be successful in everything he did.

After a while, Hezekiah became very sick and almost died. Isaiah, who was a prophet, told Hezekiah, "You are not going to get well. Tell your family you will die soon."

Hezekiah felt sad and began praying to God. "Lord, remember that I have served You with all my heart. I have done what is good." Hezekiah cried and cried.

Isaiah was in the courtyard of the palace when God gave him a message. "Go back and tell Hezekiah, 'I heard your prayer and I saw your tears, so I will heal you. I will add fifteen years to your life. I will save you and protect your city from the King of Assyria. I will do this for Myself and because of the promise I made to My servant David.'"

Then Isaiah told Hezekiah, "Crush some figs together and put the mixture of figs on your sore." Hezekiah did what Isaiah told him to do. But Hezekiah told Isaiah he wanted a sign that God was really going to heal him.

Isaiah said, "God will give you a sign. Do you want the shadow from the sun to go forward ten steps or go back ten steps?"

Hezekiah thought for a moment. "It's easy for the shadow to go forward," he said. "Make the shadow go back ten steps." So Isaiah prayed, and God made the shadow move back ten steps to where it had been before.

God had compassion on Hezekiah. He continued to rule over Judah with good health and strength. He even built a pool and dug a tunnel to bring water into the city. For the rest of his life, Hezekiah trusted God and did what was right.

God hears our prayers and sees our tears.

Focus Verse

Go back and speak to Hezekiah, the leader of my people. Tell him, "This is what the LORD, the God of your ancestor David, says: I heard your prayer and I saw your tears, so I will heal you."

2 KINGS 20:5, ERV

Talk About It

» What did Hezekiah do when Isaiah told him he was going to die?

» How did God answer Hezekiah's prayer?

» Who can you pray for who need God's healing?

DEAR GOD, thank You that You care if I am sick or sad. I know I can talk to You about anything. I know You will hear and answer me. Amen.

The Scroll in the Temple

2 Chronicles 34

JOSIAH WAS ONLY EIGHT years old when he became the king of Judah. He loved God and wanted to honor and obey Him. Some of the kings before him were not good kings. They worshiped statues of false gods, instead of worshiping the one true God. The bad kings didn't take care of God's Temple, so it fell apart. Josiah got busy! He smashed the statues. He tore down poles and altars and crushed them into dust. He got rid of everything in the kingdom that did not honor God.

Then Josiah hired workers to fix up the Temple. While they were working, a priest named Hilkiah found the Book of the Law that Moses had written on a scroll. The workmen brought the book to King Josiah and read it out loud.

As Josiah listened, he started crying. He was so upset that he tore his clothes. "We have not been doing what this scroll says we must do!" he said. "We must only worship the one true God!"

Josiah's men talked to a prophetess in Jerusalem named Huldah. She gave them a message from God. The Lord says, "I will bring trouble to this place and the people living here because of what they have done. But tell the king of Judah, 'You were sorry and humbled yourself before Me when you heard My words. You even tore your clothes and cried to show how sorry you are. Because your heart was tender, I have heard you and you will not see the troubles I will bring to these people.'"

Then Josiah went to the Temple and called all the people of Judah together. Everyone came, from the oldest to the youngest. The people listened as King Josiah read God's words from the scroll. Josiah promised to obey the Lord and asked the people to make the same promise. For the rest of Josiah's life, the people worshiped the one true God.

God has mercy when people are sorry
for doing wrong.

94

Talk About It

» Why did the Temple need to be fixed?

» What did Josiah do when he heard the words from the scroll?

» What does this Bible story teach you about God's mercy?

LET'S PRAY

DEAR GOD, help me to keep following You and doing what is right. Thank You for Your mercy and forgiveness. Amen.

Far from Home

Daniel 1-2, 5-6

Daniel was a teenager in the royal family of Israel. He knew God's laws and obeyed them.

One day, a mighty army from Babylon invaded Jerusalem and stole many valuable things. The king of Babylon, Nebuchadnezzar, had told his soldiers, "Bring strong, smart, handsome young men from Judah to serve in my palace." So the soldiers kidnapped Daniel and other young men and took them to Babylon, a country far from home.

The Babylonian officials gave Daniel a new name. They wanted him to forget who he used to be. They forced Daniel to learn the language, religion, and history of Babylon. They tried to make Daniel forget about God.

Daniel chose to obey God's laws, no matter what happened to him. Many times, laws were passed to stop Daniel from worshiping God, but he prayed to God anyway. He was respectful to the Babylonian leaders, but he did not worship their gods.

When the guards told Daniel to eat food sacrificed to their idols, Daniel asked if he could eat vegetables instead. After ten days, Daniel looked healthier than the young men who ate the royal food, so the guards let Daniel eat vegetables every day.

One night, King Nebuchadnezzar had a dream no one could interpret. Daniel prayed and asked God to help him understand the king's dream. Years later, when another king named Belshazzar saw a mysterious message on the wall, Daniel said the words were a message from God, and he told the king what the message was.

When Darius became the new king, he passed a law that made everyone pray to him. Daniel prayed to God anyway. He was thrown into a den of hungry lions, but Daniel kept praying, and the lions never hurt him.

Daniel praised God for giving him wisdom and knowledge to understand dreams and messages that no one else could understand. He said:

"May God be praised for ever and ever!
He is wise and powerful...
He gives knowledge to those who have understanding.
He explains deep and hidden things.
He knows what happens in the darkest places.
And where He is, everything is light."

DANIEL 2:20-22, NLT

Every time Daniel's life was in danger for obeying God, God protected Daniel and helped him to be brave. Daniel became a great leader in Babylon. He even showed kings how to follow God.

God gave Daniel wisdom and kept him safe wherever he went.

Focus Verse

God of my people of long ago, I thank and praise You. You have given me wisdom and power. You have made known to me what we asked You for.

DANIEL 2:23, NIRV

Talk About It

» What terrible thing happened to Daniel when he was a teenager?

» Why did Daniel stay faithful to God?

» How can you stand up for Jesus wherever you are?

LET'S PRAY

DEAR GOD, help me understand what You want for me. Help me stand up for truth in a kind and respectful way. I want to be brave for You. Amen.

Standing in the Fire

Daniel 3

DANIEL HAD THREE FRIENDS who were captured with him and taken to Babylon. Their Jewish names were Hananiah, Mishael, and Azariah, but the Babylonians changed their names to Shadrach, Meshach, and Abednego. God gave them wisdom and helped them become great leaders. Like Daniel, they loved and obeyed God and only prayed to Him.

One day, King Nebuchadnezzar ordered his men to make a gold statue that was ninety feet high. It

100

was tall enough for everyone in the city to see. Then Nebuchadnezzar made a law that whenever music played, everyone would bow down to his statue and honor him as a god. Anyone who refused would be burned in a furnace.

When the music played, Shadrach, Meshach, and Abednego kept standing. They knew they couldn't worship anything or anyone except God. The Babylonian leaders ran to Nebuchadnezzar and told him the men had disobeyed his law.

"Is it true that you won't bow to my statue? Don't you know I can throw you in the fire?" the king yelled at them.

"Yes, King," they replied. "It's true. But our God can save us from the fire if He wants to. We will not bow down to you. We only worship the one true God."

Nebuchadnezzar screamed in anger, "Make the fire seven times hotter! Tie them up and throw them in it!"

The guards made the fire hotter and threw Shadrach, Meshach, and Abednego into the furnace. Flames crack-led all around them as their feet walked across hot coals. Smoke hung everywhere. But the three men did not feel hot at all.

Suddenly, a man in a white robe walked with them in the fire. Nebuchadnezzar looked in the furnace and saw four men walking around! "Didn't we throw three men in the fire? I see four, and one looks like an angel!" The king shouted, "Come out! Come out!"

Shadrach, Meshach, and Abednego walked out of the furnace. The man in white had disappeared. The king's men gathered around them, smelling their clothes and hair. The friends were not burned, and they didn't even smell like smoke!

"Praise the God of Shadrach, Meshach, and Abednego Who sent His angel to protect them!" said the king. "They trusted in their God and were willing to give up their lives for Him. No one in Babylon will be allowed to speak against their God." Then the king let them rule over other leaders.

God protects those who stand up for Him.

Focus Verse

"The God we serve is able to bring us out of it alive. He will save us from your power."

DANIEL 3:17, NIRV

Talk About It

» Why were Shadrach, Meshach, and Abednego thrown into a furnace of fire?

» Who joined them in the fire?

» How can you stand up for God when someone tells you to do something you know is wrong?

LET'S PRAY

Dear God, thank You for being with me, no matter what happens. Help me to trust You more than I trust anyone else. Amen.

Runaway Prophet

Jonah 1-3

JONAH WAS A PROPHET of God. One day God gave him a message: "Get up, go to the great city of Nineveh and preach against it. I see the evil things they do." But Jonah didn't listen to God and tried to run away. He bought a ticket and got on a ship that was sailing the other direction.

Jonah found a quiet spot in the bottom of the ship and fell asleep. While he was sleeping, God sent strong winds to blow across the sea. Giant waves rocked the boat up and down. Water splashed over

the sides of the boat. The sailors were afraid the boat would break into pieces.

The sailors prayed to their false gods, but the storm did not stop. They woke up Jonah and said, "What have you done to cause this terrible storm? Pray to your God, and maybe He will save us."

Jonah told the sailors, "This storm is my fault because I'm running away from God. Throw me into the sea, and the storm will stop."

The sailors tried to row back to shore, but the storm grew stronger. Finally, the sailors threw Jonah into the sea. The storm stopped at once.

God did not forget about Jonah. As Jonah sank to the bottom, God sent a giant fish to swallow Jonah in one big gulp. For three days, Jonah prayed to God from inside the stinky belly of the fish. Then God caused the fish to swim to shore and spit Jonah out.

Once again, God told Jonah to go to Nineveh. This time Jonah went. He walked through the city shouting, "After forty days, Nineveh will be destroyed!"

When the king of Nineveh heard this, he called the people together. He told everyone to stop doing bad things. The king said, "People should cry loudly to God. Everyone must turn away from his evil life. Everyone must stop doing harm."

When God saw the people were sorry for the wrong things they were doing, He decided not to destroy the city. God gave Jonah a second chance to obey Him, and He gave the people of Nineveh a second chance to obey Him too.

God gives people second chances.

Focus Verse

God saw what the people did. He saw that they stopped doing evil things. So God changed His mind and did not do what he had warned. He did not punish them.

JONAH 3:10, ICB

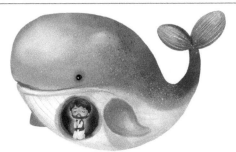

Talk About It

» What did Jonah do when God told him to go to Nineveh?

» What happened to Jonah?

» How does this story show us God's love and mercy?

LET'S PRAY

DEAR GOD, I am so glad You give people second chances when they do not listen to You. Help me to listen the first time. Amen.

A Baby and a Star

Luke 1-2

MARY WAS A TEENAGE GIRL who lived in the town of Nazareth. One day, God sent an angel to give Mary a message. "Greetings!" said the angel. "The Lord is with you. You are special to Him."

Mary was surprised and confused. "What does this mean?" she wondered.

The angel said, "Don't be afraid, Mary, because God is pleased with you. You're going to have a baby boy, and you will name Him Jesus. He will be great.

People will call Him the Son of the Most High God. He will be a king like His ancestor David, and His kingdom will never end."

Mary was even more confused. "How can this be?" she asked.

The angel explained that the power of the Holy Spirit would make this happen.

Mary believed what the angel told her. "I am the Lord's servant," she said.

When Mary was almost ready to have her baby, she traveled with her husband, Joseph, to the town of Bethlehem where Joseph's family lived. The Roman ruler wanted to count the people in his kingdom. This was all part of God's plan because many years earlier, the prophet Micah said the Ruler of Israel would come from Bethlehem.

Mary and Joseph arrived in Bethlehem, but they could not find a place to stay. They spent the night sleeping near the animals. When Mary's baby was born, she wrapped Him in strips of cloth and placed Him in a manger.

Meanwhile, some shepherds were out in the fields watching over their sheep. Suddenly the sky became bright, and an angel appeared. The shepherds were terrified!

"Don't be afraid," said the angel. "I have great news! The Savior was born in Bethlehem. He is the

Messiah! You will find Him wrapped in strips of cloth and lying in a manger." Then angels filled the sky saying, "Praise God in heaven! Peace on earth!"

The shepherds ran quickly and found Jesus in the manger, just like the angel had said. After seeing the baby, the shepherds were so excited they praised God and told everyone what had happened.

That night, God placed a special star in the sky to let the whole world know He sent His Son to earth. Jesus is God's plan to save the world from sin and show everyone how much He loves us.

God loves us so much that He sent His Son Jesus to earth.

Focus Verse

"Today your Savior was born in David's town. He is the Messiah, the Lord."

LUKE 2:11, ERV

Talk About It

» What news did the angel give to Mary?

» Why was Jesus born in Bethlehem?

» Why is it important that God sent Jesus to earth?

LET'S PRAY

DEAR GOD, thank You for sending Your Son Jesus to the world to show how much You love me. Amen.

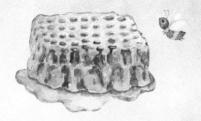

Grasshoppers and Honey

Matthew 3; John 1

A MAN NAMED JOHN lived in the wilderness, where he ate grasshoppers and wild honey for dinner. He wore clothes made from camel's hair and tied a leather belt around his waist. People thought he was a little weird, but God had a special purpose for John's life. God wanted John to help people get ready for Jesus.

People from all over Judea would come to see John and listen to him preach. John told the people, "Repent of your sins and turn to God, for the Kingdom of Heaven is near." After people were sorry for their sins and turned back to God, John baptized them in the Jordan River.

One day, Jesus went to the river and asked John to baptize Him. But John said, "I am the one who needs to be baptized by You." Jesus explained it was God's plan for John to baptize Him, so John agreed.

After John baptized Jesus, the clouds opened, and the Spirit of God came in the form of a dove and rested on Jesus. A voice from heaven said, "This is My dearly loved Son, Who brings Me great joy."

John became known as John the Baptist. Some of the Jewish leaders didn't understand who he was. "Are you the prophet Elijah?" they asked. "Are you the Messiah?"

John answered, "I am not a prophet, and I am not the Messiah." When John saw Jesus coming toward them, he said, "He is the one I was talking about when I said, 'A man is coming after me Who is far greater than I am, for He existed long before me.'"

John was a humble man. John knew Jesus was the Son of God, the Messiah, Who had come down from heaven. John cared about people and wanted them to follow Jesus instead of him. John spent his whole life telling others Jesus was the Messiah they were waiting for.

John the Baptist was a humble man who wanted people to follow Jesus.

Focus Verse

The next day John saw Jesus coming toward him and said, "Look! The Lamb of God who takes away the sin of the world!"

JOHN 1:29, NLT

Talk About It

» What food did John eat in the wilderness?

» Why did John want people to follow Jesus?

» How can you follow Jesus?

LET'S PRAY

DEAR GOD, help me to follow You every day. Help me to tell others about You. Amen.

Jesus' Best Friends

Matthew 4,10; Mark 6:6-12; Luke 5:1-11; John 1:35-51

JESUS BEGAN INVITING people to be His friends and helpers. He wanted to teach them how to love God better and love one another. One day, Jesus went walking along the Sea of Galilee, near His hometown. He saw two brothers fishing with a net. Their names were Simon Peter and Andrew. Jesus walked a little farther and saw two more brothers who were fixing their nets.

"Come and follow me," Jesus said. "I will send you out to fish for people."

The four fishermen left their nets and followed Jesus.

The next day Jesus met a man named Philip and said, "Come, follow Me." Philip looked for his friend Nathanael and told him about Jesus. So, Philip and Nathanael both followed Jesus. Jesus asked Thomas, Thaddeus, and another James to be his followers. He also called Judas and Judas Iscariot. Then He invited Simon the Zealot and Matthew. These men became Jesus' twelve disciples. They followed Jesus wherever He went. They listened to Him teach and watched Him do many miracles.

Jesus told them, "Go and tell people the Kingdom of Heaven is near. Heal the sick, raise the dead, cure those with skin diseases, and cast out demons. Give as freely as you have received!"

The disciples stared at each other. They couldn't do those things! How could they ever talk to all the people who needed Jesus?

But Jesus just smiled at them. He said, "The harvest is huge. But there are only a few workers. Ask the Lord of the harvest to send workers out into His harvest field."

Jesus invited women to follow Him, too. Mary Magdalene, Susanna, Joanna, and Salome all helped

Jesus by sharing their money and time. Jesus' mother also followed Him and loved hearing Him teach.

Wherever Jesus went, the disciples helped Him. They listened to His stories and asked Him questions. Jesus told them, "No one has greater love than the one who gives their life for their friends. You are my friends if you do what I command."

Jesus wanted all people to know about God's love and compassion. He wanted to take away people's sadness and pain. His friends would help Him finish the job God gave Him to do.

Jesus invited friends to follow Him and
tell everyone about God's love.

118

Focus Verse

"Come, follow Me," Jesus said.
"I will send you out to fish for people."

MATTHEW 4:19, NIRV

Talk About It

» How were Jesus' friends different from each other? How were they alike?

» What did Jesus say to make people follow Him and become His friends?

» How can you bring your friends to Jesus?

LET'S PRAY

DEAR GOD, thank You for asking me to be Your friend. I want to follow You and obey You all my life. Help me to invite my friends to follow Jesus too. Amen.

A New Friend

John 4

Jesus and His disciples traveled from town to town, meeting new people and telling them about God's love. One day, Jesus took His disciples through a town called Samaria. Jesus sat at the well and sent His friends into town to buy lunch. Jesus wanted to wait and meet someone new.

While Jesus sat next to the well, a woman came with her bucket to draw water.

"Will you give me a drink?" Jesus asked her.

The woman looked surprised. "Why are you talking to me? The Jews and the Samaritans aren't friends."

"If you knew Who I was," Jesus said, "You'd ask Me for a drink."

"You don't even have a bucket," she said.

Jesus smiled. "That's true. But I'm talking about what your soul needs, not what your body wants. If you accept what I'm offering, you'll never be thirsty again. I'm offering eternal life."

"I'd love that kind of water," she said. "I'm tired of coming here to the well."

"Go call your husband," Jesus said. "Let's talk to him."

The woman looked down, embarrassed. "I don't have a husband."

"I know," Jesus said. "You've had five husbands, and you don't have one now."

The woman blushed. "Sir, you must be a prophet! You know, I want to worship God. I believe the Savior is coming."

Jesus looked at her tenderly. "I am the Savior," He said. "God calls people to worship Him. He speaks the truth about Me."

The woman's face glowed with excitement. "Wait right here!" she said. She left her bucket at the well and ran back into town. "Everyone, come with me!" she shouted. "I just met a friend Who knows everything about me. I think this is the Savior! God has come to save us from our sins!"

While the woman was gone, Jesus' disciples returned with food for lunch. "Eat something, Teacher. You must be hungry."

"I have already been filled," Jesus said. "My food is to do God's work. Look around you. People are ready and waiting to accept God's love. We just have to tell them."

Many people in Samaria believed in Jesus because of the woman's story. They said, "Now we believe because we have seen for ourselves that He is the Savior of the world."

Jesus made friends so He could tell them
how to be saved from their sins.

First we believed in Jesus because of what You told us. But now we believe because we heard Him ourselves. We know that this man really is the Savior of the world.

JOHN 4:42, ICB

Talk About It

» Why did Jesus sit at the well in Samaria?

» What did Jesus offer the woman at the well?

» Why do people believe in Jesus today?

LET'S PRAY

DEAR GOD, thank You for being the Savior of the world. I believe in You. Help me to tell others about Your love. Amen.

Blessed People

Matthew 5:1-6, 6:1-4

LOTS OF PEOPLE followed Jesus wherever He went. One day, there were so many people around Jesus, that He went up the side of a mountain so everyone could see Him. Jesus talked to them for a long time that day. He taught them how to live so they would be happy and blessed.

Jesus taught these things:

"God blesses people who are poor and know they need Him. The Kingdom of Heaven is theirs.

God blesses people who are sad. He will comfort them.

God blesses people who are humble. The whole earth will be theirs.

God blesses people who want to do what's right.
He will make them happy doing right.

God blesses people who show mercy to others.
God will show mercy to them.

God blesses people whose hearts are pure.
They will see God.

God blesses those who work for peace.
They will be called children of God.

God blesses people who are treated badly for doing
what is right. The Kingdom of Heaven is theirs.

God blesses you when people are mean to you for
being My followers. Be happy because you will
get a reward in heaven."

Jesus wanted the people to understand God would bless them for being kind and loving toward others. He called His followers "the salt of the earth." The people knew salt kept their food from spoiling and made it taste better. Following Jesus would also make their lives better.

Jesus told His followers, "You are the light of the world—like a city on a hilltop that cannot be hidden." Jesus told people to shine like lights so everyone could see Jesus living inside of them.

Jesus also talked about giving to others who had a need. He said when they gave, they should not let everyone know, but to do it quietly. Even though others may not see what they give, God promised to bless them.

Jesus wanted the people to understand that even though obeying God's law was important, treating people with love and kindness was the best way to receive God's blessings.

God blesses people who care about others.

Focus Verse

One day as He saw the crowds gathering, Jesus went up on the mountainside and sat down. His disciples gathered around Him, and He began to teach them.

MATTHEW 5:1-2, NLT

Talk About It

» Why did Jesus go up a mountainside to talk to the people?

» Why does God want us to be kind to others?

» How can you be kind to someone today?

LET'S PRAY

Dear God, thank You for teaching me how to live and to treat others with love and kindness. Amen.

Born Again

John 3

NICODEMUS WAS a wise, old man. He was a Pharisee, who was one of the important religious leaders for the Jewish people. He had spent all his life studying God's Word. Nicodemus knew Jesus had God's power. Nobody but Jesus could heal sick people or make blind people see. Jesus taught Scripture with a special understanding. Nicodemus wanted to find out everything about Jesus.

But Nicodemus was afraid of what his Pharisee friends would think if he followed Jesus. One dark night, after everyone else was sleeping, Nicodemus visited Jesus so he could ask Him questions. Nicodemus was nervous and embarrassed, but Jesus just smiled at him. "Teacher," said Nicodemus, "I know that God has sent You, because no one can do miracles like You're doing unless God sent Him."

"Yes. No one can even see the kingdom of God unless they are born again," Jesus answered.

Nicodemus scratched his head. "But I am an old man. How can I go back inside my mother and be born again?"

Jesus said, "You are talking about a physical birth. I am talking about a spiritual birth. You are not just a body. You have a soul. And your soul wants to know God. It wants to be re-born. That's why God reaches out to you."

Nicodemus didn't understand.

Jesus continued, "God so loved the world that He gave His one and only Son. Anyone who believes in Him will not die but will have eternal life. God did not send His Son into the world to judge the world. He sent His Son to save the world through Him."

Nicodemus thought about Jesus' words. If God wanted to forgive sins, that meant He would send His Son to earth. Jesus was doing all the miracles that only God could do. Did that mean Jesus was the Son of God?

Nicodemus went away and thought about everything Jesus said. He watched what Jesus did every day. When his Pharisee friends got angry and jealous of Jesus' power, Nicodemus said, "Let's talk to Jesus. Let's watch Him. His actions will prove if He is from God or not."

Nicodemus liked talking to Jesus and he wanted to follow Him. But he was afraid to tell his friends how much he wanted to know Jesus.

Jesus wanted Nicodemus to ask questions so he could understand why Jesus came.

Focus Verse

God so loved the world that He gave
His one and only Son. Anyone who
believes in Him will not die but will have
eternal life. God did not send His Son into
the world to judge the world. He sent His
Son to save the world through Him.

JOHN 3:16-17, NIRV

Talk About It

» Why did Nicodemus visit Jesus in the middle of the night?

» What did Jesus mean by being "born again"?

» Why should you be "born again"?

DEAR GOD, thank You for sending Jesus to save me from my sins. I believe Jesus is Your Son, and He can save me. Please come into my heart and forgive my sins. Amen.

LET'S PRAY

The Good Neighbor

Luke 10:25-37

MANY JEWISH LEADERS were jealous of Jesus' popularity. They felt embarrassed that Jesus knew more about God than they did. So one day, a teacher of the law tried to trick Jesus with a question. "What must I do to have eternal life?" he asked.

Jesus answered the teacher with a question. "What is written in the law? What do you read there?"

The man said, "Love the Lord Your God with all your heart, all your soul, and your strength, and all your mind. And love your neighbor as you love yourself."

"Your answer is right," said Jesus.

"But who is my neighbor?" asked the teacher.

Jesus answered the man's question by telling a story, called a parable.

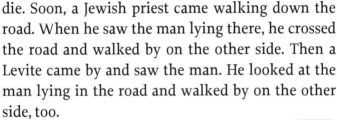

"A man was traveling down the road to Jericho when some robbers attacked him. They tore off his clothes and beat him. Then the robbers left him in the road to die. Soon, a Jewish priest came walking down the road. When he saw the man lying there, he crossed the road and walked by on the other side. Then a Levite came by and saw the man. He looked at the man lying in the road and walked by on the other side, too.

"After a while, a Samaritan traveled along the road and saw the man who was hurt. The Samaritan felt sorry for the man and stopped to help him. The Samaritan poured oil and wine on the man's sores. He put the man on his own donkey and took

him to an inn. The Samaritan gave the innkeeper two silver coins and told him to take care of the man. The Samaritan said, 'If you spend more money on him, I will pay you when I come back again.'"

Jesus looked at the teacher and asked, "Which of these three men was a neighbor to the man who was attacked?"

The teacher of the law answered, "The one who helped the man."

Jesus said, "Then go and do the same thing he did!" Jesus wanted everyone to understand that taking care of others is a way to be a good neighbor.

Jesus taught others how to love everyone.

Focus Verse

The man answered,
"You must love the LORD your God
with all your heart, all your soul,
all your strength, and all your mind."
And, "Love your neighbor as yourself."

LUKE 10:27, NLT

Talk About It

» How did the teacher try to trick Jesus?

» Who acted like a neighbor to the man who was hurt?

» Who is your neighbor?

LET'S PRAY

DEAR GOD, help me to notice people who need my help. I want to be a good neighbor to everyone. Amen.

A Doctor for Everyone

Matthew 9; Mark 3; Luke 8

ONE DAY A MAN went to see Jesus. His four friends carried him on a mat because he couldn't walk. When they arrived at the house where Jesus was teaching, they saw a crowd looking in through the doors and windows, trying to hear what Jesus was saying. The house was packed with people standing shoulder-to-shoulder.

"I'll never get in," said the man on the mat.

"Don't worry," said his friends. They carried him up the outside stairs to the rooftop. Setting him down, they carefully pulled away all the straw and clay that made up the roof until they had made a big hole. Then they lowered their friend on the mat, right in front of Jesus! The people in the house were so surprised!

Jesus smiled and told the man, "Your sins are forgiven. Take up your bed and walk."

The man stood up. He jumped up and down. His legs worked!

Later, Jesus met a blind man and rubbed mud on his eyes and healed him from blindness. For the first time in his life, the man saw the blue sky, lots of people, and colorful trees. He was overjoyed!

Another time, Jesus met a man with a shriveled hand. The man hid his hand inside his coat so people wouldn't see it. "Stretch out your hand," Jesus told him. Immediately, the man's hand was whole again.

As Jesus walked toward a village one day, ten men who had sores on their skin asked Jesus to heal them. The men had a disease called leprosy. Jesus told them to walk to the Temple. As they walked, their skin became clear again. Only one man, who was from another town, ran back and told Jesus, "Thank you."

The news of Jesus' healing power spread quickly. In a big crowd in Capernaum, a lonely woman tried to get close to Jesus. She had spent all her money on doctors but none of them could find a cure for her sickness. Believing she could be healed if she touched Jesus' robe, she pressed through the crowd until she stood behind Him.

Even though Jesus was being pushed by many people, He felt the woman touch His robe. He turned around and spoke to her. "Daughter, your faith has healed you. Go home in peace."

Everywhere Jesus went, people followed Him. They brought children who were sick, friends who couldn't walk, and neighbors who couldn't see. Jesus healed everyone who came to Him.

Jesus had compassion for everyone, so He healed all kinds of people from all kinds of problems.

Focus Verse

Jesus went through all the towns and villages. He taught in their synagogues. He preached the good news of the kingdom. And He healed every illness and sickness.

MATTHEW 9:35, NIRV

Talk About It

» What kinds of healings did Jesus do?

» Why did Jesus heal people?

» What can you do when you are sick or troubled?

DEAR GOD, I know You will take care of me. I believe You can heal me when I am sick. I will trust You and wait for Your healing. Amen.

Back to Life

Luke 7; Luke 8; John 11

BESIDES HEALING MANY people and doing amazing miracles, sometimes, Jesus raised people from the dead. He had compassion on people whose family members had died. He felt their pain and was sad with them. Once, Jesus followed a religious leader home and raised his little daughter to life. Another time, He passed a funeral procession and watched a poor widow crying after the death of her only son.

Jesus comforted her and said, "Don't cry." Then He said to her son, "Young man, get up!" The boy sat up and began to talk. Then Jesus gave the boy back to his mother, alive! Jesus loved helping people.

Jesus had some good friends who lived in a town called Bethany. Two sisters named Mary and Martha had a brother named Lazarus. They often let Jesus stay at their house. Martha made big meals for Jesus and His followers whenever they came. Mary always listened carefully to Jesus' teaching.

One day, Lazarus became sick. His sisters sent a message to Jesus, asking Him to come right away. But Jesus stayed longer in the other town until Lazarus died. He had already raised people from the dead, including a widow's only son and a religious leader's daughter. He wasn't worried about Lazarus. He had a bigger plan the sisters didn't understand.

After several days, Jesus and His friends traveled to Bethany. Martha heard He was there, so she ran down the road to meet Him, crying. "Why didn't You come earlier?" she asked. "Then Lazarus would not have died!"

"I am the resurrection and the life," Jesus said. "Do you believe in Me?"

Mary came next and asked Jesus the same thing. Then the sisters took Jesus to the tomb where Lazarus was buried. They couldn't stop crying. Jesus saw how sad everyone was. He cried with them.

Jesus prayed out loud, "Father, thank You for hearing Me. I'm saying this so everyone knows Who sent Me." Then Jesus shouted, "Lazarus, come out!"

A person wrapped like a mummy walked out of the tomb! When the people unwrapped him, it was Lazarus! He was alive!

All the people praised God for Jesus' miracle. After this, many believed Jesus was God's Son.

Jesus had the power to raise people from the dead.

Focus Verse

"I am the resurrection and the life.
Anyone who believes in Me will live,
even after dying."

JOHN 11:25-26, NLT

Talk About It

» Why were Mary and Martha crying?

» What did Jesus want to show all the people?

» What can you do when you are sad?

LET'S PRAY

DEAR GOD, I believe in You. I know You are powerful enough to give me life now, and life one day in heaven. You can do anything! Amen.

A Big Treasure

Matthew 6:19-21, 25; Matthew 13:44

JESUS AND HIS DISCIPLES didn't have a lot of money to buy things. They had to trust God to provide what they needed.

One day, Jesus was teaching in the Temple. After He finished, He and His disciples watched the people who put money into the Temple treasury. Rich people dropped in many big coins that made loud noises as they landed in the box. *Plink, plank, plunk* went the coins. Everyone could hear them give their offerings.

Then a poor woman in ragged clothes walked up to put money in the box. Her husband had died. She had no one to take care of her. She quietly dropped in two small pennies.

Jesus said to His disciples, "This poor widow has given more than everyone. They gave out of the money they had left over, but she gave everything she had to live on."

To help His friends understand how valuable it was to follow Him, Jesus told a story about a man who was digging in a field. The man's shovel hit a

hard box. He dug it up and saw it was full of coins and jewels! He quickly reburied the treasure. Then he sold everything he had so he could buy the field from the owner. He knew the field had a hidden treasure that was worth a lot of money, so when he bought the field, he was able to keep the treasure. Jesus told stories like this so His followers would understand that the kingdom of God is like a great treasure. When people follow Jesus and believe in Him, they receive a treasure that is worth more than money.

Jesus told his friends, "Don't store up treasures on earth! Moths and rust can destroy them, and thieves can break in and steal them. Instead, store up your treasures in heaven, where moths and rust cannot destroy them, and thieves cannot break in and steal them. Your heart will always be where your treasure is."

Jesus wanted people to see God's kingdom as a great treasure that He freely shares with us because He loves us.

Focus Verse

"Your heart will be where your treasure is."

MATTHEW 6:21, ERV

Talk About It

» Why do you think the woman gave all her money to the Lord?

» Why did the man buy a whole field just to get a box?

» How can you give to the Lord?

LET'S PRAY

DEAR GOD, help me to be generous with everything You've given me. Amen.

Hungry People

Matthew 14:15-21; Mark 6:30-44;
Luke 9: 10-17; John 6:1-13

JESUS AND HIS DISCIPLES wanted to be alone for a
while so they could talk and rest. They got into a
boat and crossed the Sea of Galilee. But when they
reached the shore, a large crowd was waiting for
them. Jesus felt sorry for the people and had compassion on them. He thought they were like sheep
without a shepherd. So Jesus got out of the boat and
taught them many things.

As the sun was going down, the disciples told
Jesus the people were hungry. Jesus asked His
disciple Philip, "Where can we buy bread for all
these hungry people?" Jesus already knew how He
was going to feed them, but He said this to see what
Philip would say.

"We would have to work for almost a year to have enough money to buy bread to feed all these people," said Philip. "And each person would only have a little piece."

Then Andrew brought a boy to Jesus. "Here's a boy with five loaves of barley bread and two small fish," he said. "But that's not enough food for all these people."

More than five-thousand men, plus their wives and children were in that big crowd of people. Jesus told everyone to sit down in the grass in groups of fifty or a hundred. Then Jesus took the bread in His hands and thanked God for it. As the disciples began passing the bread to the people, more and more bread appeared. There was enough bread for everyone! As Jesus passed the fish, more fish appeared! The fish never ran out! Everyone in the crowd ate the pieces of bread and fish until they were full.

Jesus told His disciples to pick up the leftover food

and put it into baskets. The disciples did what Jesus said. After they picked up the leftover food, there was enough to fill twelve big baskets! When the people saw the miracle Jesus had done, they said, "Jesus must be the Prophet we have been waiting for."

Jesus did miracles to help people.

Focus Verse

Jesus saw the huge crowd as He stepped from the boat, and He had compassion on them because they were like sheep without a shepherd. So He began teaching them many things.

MARK 6:34, NLT

Talk About It

» Why were people waiting for Jesus on the shore?

» What did Jesus do before He passed out the food?

» How does Jesus take care of you?

DEAR GOD, thank You that You care about me so much and give me everything I need. Amen.

LET'S PRAY

Lost and Found

Luke 15:11-32

ONE DAY, Jesus told three "lost-and-found" stories to help people understand God's love and compassion. The first story was about a man who had one-hundred-dred sheep. "One sheep got lost in the mountains," said Jesus. "So the shepherd left the ninety-nine sheep and looked until he found it."

Next, Jesus told a story about a woman with ten silver coins. "When she lost one coin, she cleaned every corner of her house until she found it."

Then Jesus told a story about a father who had two sons. The younger son got tired of working with his father, so he said, "Father, give me my inheritance right now."

The son's wishes made his father sad, but the father divided his money and gave half of it to the younger son. Instead of being thankful or wise, the son took the money, ran away from home, and wasted all of it.

Every day while the son was gone, the father stood looking down the road, hoping his son would come home. He wasn't angry his son had left. He only wanted him back.

Before long, the son ran out of money. He began sleeping in a pigpen, eating husks of corn left by the pigs. "I've made a terrible mistake," thought the son. "I'll go back and tell my father I'm sorry. Maybe he will let me be a servant. At least I'd have food to eat."

The son started the long walk home. He practiced what he would say. He hoped his father would let him work for him. He hoped his father wouldn't yell at him. He felt ashamed of his ragged clothing.

While the son was a long way off, his father saw him. He didn't yell at his son or remind him of the mistakes he had made. No, the father ran down the road toward his son! He grabbed him and hugged him tight.

"Father, I'm sorry," the son began to cry. "I'm not good enough to be your son anymore, but I will be your servant."

"Quick!" the father called to his servants. "Bring the best clothes for my son to wear! Put a ring on his finger! Throw a party for him! Everyone must celebrate! My son was lost, and now, he is found!"

Jesus looked around at the people. Did they understand this was how God the Father felt about them? No matter what they did or where they went, God would always watch for them to return and welcome them home.

The father forgave his son and was happy he came home.

Focus Verse

"This son of mine was dead. And now he is alive again. He was lost. And now he is found." So they began to celebrate.

LUKE 15:24, NIRV

Talk About It

» Why did the younger son leave home?

» What did the father do while the son was gone?

» How does God feel about His children?

Dear God, You are an amazing Father. Thank You for always looking for me when I wander away. Amen.

Two Stormy Nights

Matthew 14:22-33; Mark 4:35-4;
Mark 6:45-52; John 6:16-21

ONE EVENING, Jesus told His disciples, "Come with Me across the lake." So they left the crowd of people and got into a boat with Jesus. After a while, a strong wind blew across the lake. The waves splashed over the sides and filled the boat with water. The disciples were afraid and thought they would drown. They woke up Jesus, who was sleeping in the back of the boat.

"Teacher, don't you care about us? We are going to drown!" they shouted.

Jesus wanted to show them that He cared about them very much. He also wanted them to see the power God had given Him. Jesus stood up and commanded the wind and water to calm down. "Quiet! Be still!"

And just like that, the wind stopped blowing, and the waves became calm.

On another night, after Jesus had finished teaching many people, Jesus told the disciples to go to the other side of the lake and wait for Him to come. Jesus said goodbye to the people and went into the hills to pray.

Meanwhile, the disciples were in the middle of the lake, trying to row against a strong storm. The wind and waves beat against the boat. As the boat bounced up and down with the waves, Jesus walked to them on the water.

The disciples were terrified! "It's a ghost!" they cried.

But Jesus didn't want them to be scared. "Don't worry. Don't be afraid. It's Me," He said.

Peter said to Jesus, "If it's really You, Lord, tell me to come to You on the water."

"Come, Peter," said Jesus.

Peter bravely stepped out of the boat. He walked on the water toward Jesus. But when he saw the big waves and felt the strong wind, he got scared. He began sinking. "Save me, Lord!" he cried.

Jesus reached out and lifted Peter from the water. After Jesus and Peter were safely inside the boat, the wind and waves stopped. The disciples saw Jesus had power over nature. They knew for sure that Jesus was the Son of God. They knew He cared about them and didn't want them to be afraid.

Jesus cared about people who were afraid and protected them.

Focus Verse

But Jesus quickly spoke to them.
He said, "Don't worry! It's Me!
Don't be afraid."

MATTHEW 14:27, ERV

Talk About It

» What happened that made the disciples afraid?

» How did Jesus help them?

» What can you do when you are afraid?

DEAR GOD, You care when I'm afraid. Thank You for protecting me and keeping me safe. Amen.

LET'S PRAY

Expensive Perfume

Matthew 26:6-13; Mark 14:1-11; John 12:1-8

A MAN NAMED SIMON the Leper gave a dinner to honor Jesus. Simon lived in Bethany where Mary, Martha, and Lazarus lived. Jesus had healed Simon of his leprosy, so now he could live and eat with other people. Some of Jesus' friends came to Simon the Leper's house to have dinner with Jesus. Martha helped to serve the food while Lazarus sat at the table with Jesus.

Mary came into the room with a small jar of expensive perfume. Someone would have to work a whole year to earn enough money to buy it. But Mary knew that nothing was too good for her Savior. She wanted to show Jesus how much she loved Him because she knew how much Jesus loved her. She poured the perfume over Jesus' feet and wiped His feet with

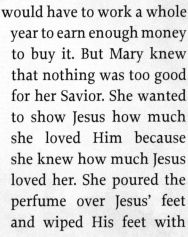

her hair. The sweet smell of perfume filled the whole house.

Judas Iscariot, who was one of Jesus' disciples, didn't like Mary's gift. He thought it was a waste of money to pour the perfume on Jesus' feet. "The perfume should have been sold and the money given to the poor," he said. But Judas didn't really care about the poor. He took care of the disciples' money and would keep some of it for himself.

Jesus spoke sternly to Judas. "Leave Mary alone," He said. "Why are you bothering her?

It was right for her to save the perfume for today. She is getting Me ready for My death and burial. You will always have poor people with you, but you will not always have Me. I tell you the truth, the Good News will be preached all over the world. People will remember what Mary has done."

Everyone was confused by Mary's gift. They hadn't understood Jesus was willing to die for the sins of the whole world. But Mary followed Jesus closely and wanted to be near Him. Mary was thankful that Jesus had raised her brother, Lazarus, from the dead and healed many people. Jesus was more precious to her than anything else in the world.

Mary loved Jesus with her whole heart and wanted to show she believed in Him.

Focus Verse

[Mary] poured the perfume on Jesus' feet, and then she wiped his feet with her hair. And the sweet smell from the perfume filled the whole house.

JOHN 12:3, ICB

Talk About It

» What did Mary do that made Judas upset?

» What did Jesus say to Judas?

» How can you show Jesus how much you love Him?

LET'S PRAY

DEAR GOD, thank You for loving me. I want You to know I love You, too. Amen.

Trying to See Jesus

Luke 19:1-10

ZACCHAEUS COLLECTED TAXES for the Roman government in his town of Jericho. Zacchaeus didn't have any friends. People didn't like him because he got rich by charging them more than they needed to pay. Then he kept the extra money for himself. Zacchaeus was a cheater.

One day, Zacchaeus heard Jesus was coming to Jericho. Zacchaeus had heard many stories about Jesus eating with sinners. Even one of Jesus' disciples had been a tax collector, like Zacchaeus. If only he could see Him! Zacchaeus wondered what kind of a preacher made friends with cheaters.

Zacchaeus ran along the road Jesus would take into town. Mobs of people lined both sides of the road. They had been standing there all day waiting for Jesus to walk by. Zacchaeus tried to elbow his way to the front so he could see, but no one would let him through.

Zacchaeus hopped up and down, but he couldn't see over anyone's head. He was a short man. No one in the crowd paid attention to him. Then Zacchaeus noticed a sycamore tree, giving shade to those who waited.

Quickly, Zacchaeus pushed toward the trunk and climbed up. He had to see Jesus!

The noise of the crowd grew louder. Jesus and His disciples were walking down the road. Jesus stopped and listened to people along the way. He walked closer to the sycamore tree. Zacchaeus could see Jesus' smile and kind eyes.

Instead of walking past the tree, Jesus stopped right under its branches and looked up. "Zacchaeus," Jesus said. "Come down quickly. Today, I'm coming to your house for dinner."

Excited and surprised, Zacchaeus lowered himself to the ground.

"Why would Jesus go home with him?" someone grumbled.

"Doesn't He know Zacchaeus is a cheater?" someone else said.

"How does Jesus even know his name?" asked another.

Zacchaeus saw Jesus' face and immediately felt sorry for all the bad things he had ever done. "Jesus, I promise You, I will give away half of my money to the poor, and if I have cheated anyone, I will repay them four times as much as I took from them!"

Jesus smiled. "Today, you have been saved. You are a true believer. This is why I have come—to seek and save the lost."

Together, Zacchaeus and Jesus walked home for dinner.

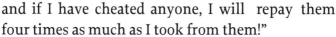

Jesus saw Zacchaeus and loved him,
even though other people didn't.

162

Focus Verse

"The Son of Man came to find lost
people and save them."

LUKE 19:10, ERV

Talk About It

» What wrong things did Zacchaeus do?

» Why did Zacchaeus climb a tree?

» How does Jesus forgive you?

LET'S PRAY

DEAR GOD, I want to follow You all my life.
Thank You for seeing me and forgiving me
when I do bad things. I am sorry for my
sins. Amen.

Washing Dirty Feet

Mark 10:41-45; John 13:1-17

JESUS AND HIS DISCIPLES traveled through many towns. The disciples watched and learned as Jesus healed people and taught them about God's love. Crowds of people followed them wherever they went. But sometimes Jesus wanted to be alone with His disciples and talk to them about why He came and what was going to happen.

Jesus and His disciples were in Jerusalem for Passover week, an important Jewish holiday. Jesus wanted to have dinner with just His disciples. He knew it was almost time for Him to go back to heaven. Jesus wanted to show His disciples how much

He loved them, but He also wanted to teach them an important lesson.

While His disciples were eating, Jesus stood up and wrapped a towel around His waist. Then He poured water into a large bowl. Jesus knelt in front of each disciple. He took off their sandals and washed their dirty feet; He dried them with the towel.

When it was Peter's turn, he said, "Lord, are You going to wash my feet? You should not wash my feet!" Peter thought that Jesus was too important to be washing feet. That was a job for servants.

Jesus told Peter, "Right now you don't understand what I am doing, but later you will understand. Unless I wash your feet, you cannot be My follower."

Then Peter said to Jesus, "Lord, don't just wash my feet, wash all of me. I want to follow You completely!"

When Jesus finished, He sat at the table with them.

"Do you understand what I have done for you?" He asked. "You are right to call me Lord and Teacher, because that is what I am. But I have washed your feet to give you an example of how to treat others. You should serve others the way I have served you."

Jesus wanted His disciples to understand if they wanted to be like Jesus, they would have to serve others. Jesus said, "Even the Son of Man did not come to be served. Instead, He came to serve others. He came to give His life as the price for setting many people free."

Even though Jesus was Lord, He served people because He loved them.

Focus Verse

"I, your Lord and Teacher, have washed your feet. So you also should wash one another's feet. I have given you an example. You should do as I have done for you."

JOHN 13:14-15, NIRV

Talk About It

» Why did Jesus wash His disciples' feet?

» What did Jesus say to Peter?

» How can you serve people that you know?

LET'S PRAY

DEAR GOD, thank You for stories in the Bible that show me how to live. Help me to serve others by loving and helping them. Amen.

A Forever Friend

Matthew 26-27; Mark 14-15; Luke 22-23; John 18-19

JESUS TAUGHT HIS DISCIPLES to love one another. He said, "That's how people will know you're My disciples. You are My friends if you obey My teaching."

During the special supper with His disciples, Jesus served them and looked at them with compassion. Then He said a hard thing to believe. "One of you will betray me."

Judas Iscariot left the meal to meet the religious leaders who hated Jesus. They paid Judas thirty pieces of silver to show them where to arrest Jesus. They had to keep it a secret because Jesus never did anything wrong!

Judas took the soldiers to a garden where Jesus was praying. It was dark out, so Judas kissed Jesus to show the soldiers which person to take. The Jewish leaders took Jesus to a courtroom that night. People told lies about Him and accused Jesus of pretending to be God.

The governor named Pilate had Jesus beaten. The crowds shouted to kill Jesus. Pilate agreed, even though he knew Jesus hadn't done anything wrong. Soldiers made Jesus carry a heavy wooden cross through Jerusalem, up a steep hill. Jesus became weak and could hardly walk. A man named Simon helped carry the cross.

The soldiers nailed Jesus' hands and feet to the wooden beams. They placed the cross into a big hole and raised it up so everyone could see Him. Jesus hung on the cross for many hours. He was in great pain.

Even though Jesus suffered, He still loved everyone. He prayed to His Father.

Jesus' mother Mary, Mary Magdalene, John, and other disciples stood near the cross crying. Jesus told His mother that John would take care of her.

Two thieves hung on crosses next to Jesus, and He comforted them too. One thief believed in Jesus, so Jesus told him they would see each other in heaven. Jesus forgave the soldiers for hurting Him.

Around noon, the sky turned black, and an earthquake shook the whole city.

Jesus cried out, "Father, I give My spirit into Your hands!" Then Jesus died.

Nicodemus, the Pharisee who believed in Jesus, quickly took Jesus' body down and wrapped it for burial. A man named Joseph owned a tomb nearby where they could bury Jesus' body. The disciples felt deep sadness and fear. Everyone went home and hid. They couldn't understand why Jesus died. They thought He was their King. They forgot Jesus had come to die for the sins of the whole world.

Jesus died to be everyone's Forever Friend and Savior.

Focus Verse

No one has greater love than the one who gives their life for their friends.

JOHN 15:13, NIRV

Talk About It

» Who turned over Jesus to the Jewish leaders?

» Why did Jesus let the soldiers kill Him?

» How did the disciples feel when Jesus died?

LET'S PRAY

Dear God, thank You for dying on the cross for my sins. I believe You are God's Son and that You love me. I want You to be my Forever Friend. Help me to love and obey You for the rest of my life. Amen.

A Sunday Surprise

Matthew 28; Mark 16; Luke 24; John 20

EARLY SUNDAY MORNING, Mary Magdalene, Salome, Joanna, Mary, and other women went to the tomb with spices to put on Jesus' body. They hoped the soldiers guarding the tomb would let them inside. The Jewish leaders remembered Jesus had raised Lazarus from the dead. They were worried that Jesus' disciples would steal His body and say that He was alive.

Suddenly, an earthquake shook the ground. A bright angel came down from heaven, rolled back the stone, and sat on it. The guards fell over like they were dead. The women were surprised and frightened.

"Don't be afraid," said the angel. "I know you are looking for Jesus, who was killed. He is not here. He has risen from the dead, just like He said. Go quickly and tell His disciples."

The women ran to share the surprising news. Peter, John, and Mary Magdalene came back to the tomb and looked inside. When John went inside, he saw it was empty! Jesus' body was not there!

Mary stayed at the tomb, crying. She felt sad and confused. "Why are you crying?" the angels asked her.

"I don't know where they took my Lord," she said.

"Mary," came a voice behind her.

She turned and saw Jesus! He was alive!

"Teacher!" she cried.

That evening, as the disciples hid in a locked room, Jesus walked right through the door! "Peace be with you!" He said. The disciples worshiped Him. They finally understood He had died to pay for their sins.

Jesus stayed and ate dinner with His friends. He came another time and spoke to Thomas, who couldn't believe the news until he saw Jesus for himself. Jesus also met with Peter. "Follow me," Jesus said, just like He had told Peter when they first met years before. "You are my messenger to tell the Good News." Jesus appeared to hundreds of other people to prove He was alive again.

Then Jesus gathered His disciples on a hilltop. "Go and tell everyone the Good News. Make disciples. I will never leave you. I am with you forever, even until the end of the world." Then He rose into the sky and disappeared behind a cloud.

Jesus had power over death so everyone who believed in Him could have a forever life with Him in heaven.

Focus Verse

"He is not here. He has risen,
just as He said He would."

MATTHEW 28:6, NIRV

Talk About It

» What surprises did the women find at
Jesus' tomb?

» How did Jesus show compassion to His
friends who were sad?

» How can you have a forever life with Jesus?

LET'S PRAY

DEAR GOD, thank You for saving me from
my sins and living inside of me. I'm so
happy I never have to be alone! Amen.

Better Than Silver or Gold

Acts 3:1-16

AFTER JESUS WENT back to heaven, God gave the disciples power through the Holy Spirit to teach and heal people, so they could continue the work Jesus had started.

One afternoon, Peter and John went to the Temple for a prayer service. As they walked by the Temple gate, they noticed a man sitting on the ground. He couldn't walk, so every day someone would bring him there so he could beg people for money. When the man saw Peter and John, he called out to them.

Peter and John looked at the man. "Look at us!" said Peter. The man got excited because he was sure Peter and John were going to give him some money. But Peter said, "I don't have any silver or gold for you. But I'll give you what I have. In the name of Jesus Christ, get up and walk!"

Peter reached out his hand and helped the man stand up. Suddenly, the man's feet and ankles became strong, and he began to walk. Then he jumped up and down, praising God!

When the man walked into the Temple with Peter and John, the people were surprised and confused. They knew he was the man who sat and begged at the gate every day. They had walked past him many times. And now, here he was—standing on his own two feet, smiling and praising God!

Peter saw the people looking at them. "Why are you surprised?" he asked. "Why are you staring at us? We are not the ones who made this man walk. God gave us the power in the name of Jesus to heal him. It was through faith in Jesus that he was healed. You know he could not walk, but now you can see with your own eyes that he is healed."

The disciples helped people who were sick and sad. They wanted all people to believe Jesus was the Son of God Who had come to bring hope to the world and save people from sin.

Peter and John healed people through Jesus' power.

Focus Verse

But Peter said, "I don't have any silver or gold for you. But I'll give you what I have. In the name of Jesus Christ, the Nazarene, get up and walk!"

ACTS 3:6, NLT

Talk About It

» Why did the man who couldn't walk sit by the Temple gate every day?

» What did Peter say when the man asked for money?

» What can you give that would help someone else?

DEAR GOD, thank You that You can do amazing things for people because You are so powerful. Amen.

LET'S PRAY

Clothes for the Poor

Acts 9:32-42

PETER TRAVELED to the town of Lydda to spend time with the believers who lived there. He met a man named Aeneas who couldn't walk. Peter said to him, "Aeneas! Jesus Christ heals you! Get up and roll up your mat!" Aeneas was healed and got up right away. The people who saw this miracle were amazed and believed in Jesus.

Not too far away, in the town of Joppa, lived a woman named Tabitha. She was also called Dorcas. She believed in Jesus and spent her life helping the poor and sewing clothes. She made beautiful robes and clothing for people who needed them.

One day, Tabitha got sick and died. The believers in Joppa had heard how Peter healed the man in Lydda, so they sent two men to Lydda to find Peter. "Please come with us to Joppa right away!" they begged.

Peter went to Joppa with the two men. When they came to Tabitha's home, the women took Peter to an upstairs room where they had put Tabitha's body. The women cried as they showed Peter what Tabitha had made before she died. "Look at these beautiful robes and clothes," the women said with tears in their eyes.

Peter could see that Tabitha had been a kind woman. He understood why her friends loved her so much. He felt sad for them. "Please leave the room," he told them.

When Peter was alone in the room, he got on his knees and prayed. He turned toward Tabitha and said, "Tabitha, get up!" She opened her eyes right away. When she saw Peter, she sat up. Peter took Tabitha by the hand and helped her stand up. Then he brought Tabitha to her friends so they could see she was alive.

Many more people believed in Jesus when they heard what had happened. Jesus' helpers carried on the work Jesus had started by healing and helping others and telling them how to be saved. Many new followers, like Tabitha, showed God's love through their kindness toward others. Tabitha spread God's love to everyone in Joppa.

When we become more like Jesus,
we have compassion for others.

Talk About It

» Why did two men go to Lydda to find Peter?

» What was Tabitha known for?

» How does following Jesus help us have
compassion for others.

LET'S PRAY

DEAR GOD, help me to become more like
Jesus and to care about others. Amen.

Everyone Is Welcome

Acts 10

A ROMAN COMMANDER named Cornelius lived in Caesarea. Although he was not a Jew, he loved God and served Him. He gave money to the poor and prayed to God often. One day, an angel appeared and spoke to Cornelius.

The angel said, "Cornelius, God sees your kindness to the poor and hears your prayers. Send to Joppa for a man named Peter. He is staying with Simon the tanner, who lives by the sea."

Cornelius didn't understand what was happening, but right away, he sent three men to find Peter and bring him for a visit.

Meanwhile, Peter was praying on the top of Simon the tanner's house. He was hungry and waiting for his lunch. Peter had an unusual vision. He saw a sheet being lowered from the sky, full of animals he was not allowed to eat, according to Jewish laws. But while the sheet hung in front of him, Peter heard a voice say, "Get up, Peter. Kill and eat the animals."

This happened three times. Even though his stomach was growling, each time Peter said, "No, Lord, I can't eat these kinds of animals because they are unclean."

Each time, the voice said, "Anything that God makes clean is good."

Then the sheet rose back into the sky, and Peter heard *knock-knock* at Simon's front door. Simon called up to him, "Peter, three men are here to meet you."

Peter walked downstairs to meet them.

"We are from Cornelius," they said. "He is a Roman commander, who loves God. An angel sent us to get you so we could hear what you have to say about God."

Since Jesus' death, none of the disciples had preached the Good News to anyone except Jews. The Jews did not invite other people into their homes or talk to them. But Peter invited the men inside, and then he went with them to meet Cornelius. Peter told Cornelius and his friends all about the sheet full of animals. "God has shown me the Good News of Jesus is for everyone. Jesus wants every person to know Him and be filled with His Spirit."

Everyone in the house was filled with God's Spirit. Then Peter baptized all of them.

God showed Peter that He wanted to share His love with everyone.

Focus Verse

I really understand now that God does not consider some people to be better than others. He accepts anyone who worships Him and does what is right. It is not important what nation they come from.

ACTS 10:35, ERV

Talk About It

» Who told Cornelius to send for Peter?

» Why did God show Peter a sheet full of animals?

» Does God love any group of people more than others?

LET'S PRAY

DEAR GOD, help me not to be proud or unkind to anyone. I want to include everyone and tell them about Your love. Amen.

Singing in Jail

Acts 16:16-40

PAUL AND SILAS traveled to many different places to tell everyone about Jesus. In Greece, they were going to a prayer meeting when they met a slave girl who had a bad spirit in her. The spirit gave the girl power to know about things that would happen in the future. But she wasn't a prophet from God, so her words were not messages from God. The people who owned the slave girl didn't care about her. They just wanted to make money off her.

The girl followed Paul and Silas around for many days. Paul was bothered by the bad spirit inside of her. He said to the spirit, "By the power of Jesus Christ, I command you to come out of her!" As soon as he said those words, the spirit came out of the girl.

The girl was happy to be free from the bad spirit, but her owners were angry. Now they couldn't make money from her fortune-telling. The girl's owners grabbed Paul and Silas and dragged them to the city rulers in the marketplace. "Paul and

Silas are causing trouble in our city!" the owners said. The rulers gave an order to have Paul and Silas beaten and thrown into prison.

Their hands and feet were bound with chains in their prison cell so they could not get away. Around midnight, Paul and Silas prayed and sang praises to God. The other prisoners listened. They were surprised by the joy that Paul and Silas had.

Suddenly, a big earthquake shook the ground. The prison gates flew open, and all the prisoners' chains fell off. The jailer shook with fear. He knew he would be killed if the prisoners escaped.

Paul called out to the jailer, "Don't worry! We are all here!"

The jailor brought Paul and Silas out of prison. Still shaking, the jailer asked, "Sirs, what should I do to be saved?"

Paul and Silas replied, "Believe in the Lord Jesus, and you will be saved!"

The jailer believed, and so did the people who were with him. Paul baptized the jailer and everyone who was in his house. Then the jailer washed Paul and Silas' wounds and gave them something to eat.

Even though Paul and Silas were treated badly,
they cared about the jailer and wanted
him to know Jesus.

Focus Verse

About midnight Paul and Silas were praying and singing songs to God. The other prisoners were listening to them.

ACTS 16:25, ICB

Talk About It

» Why were Paul and Silas thrown into prison?

» What important question did the jailer ask Paul and Silas?

» Why is it important to praise God when we are having a hard day?

DEAR GOD, You love me so much! I am saved from sin by believing in You. Help me to sing and pray, even on days that are hard. Amen.

LET'S PRAY

Second Chances

Acts 2:32-36; Acts 9:22-29, 13:1-3, 15:36-40;
Colossians 4:10; 2 Timothy 4:11; 1 Peter 5:13

BARNABAS WAS A LEADER and teacher in the early church. One day a man came to church who was famous for killing Jesus' followers. When he said he wanted to join their church, everyone was terrified!

But Barnabas put his arm around the man's shoulders. He said, "Haven't you heard how this man Saul met Jesus on the road to Damascus? He's become a believer, just like us. Let's welcome him into the church. Everyone deserves a second chance."

Barnabas became Saul's best friend. He taught him all about following Jesus and gave him opportunities to preach in a few churches. Before long, the church in Antioch sent Barnabas and Saul out as missionaries to other countries.

Barnabas took his young relative John-Mark with them so he could learn about sharing the gospel. The group of friends went everywhere, telling people about God's love and Jesus' death and resurrection. Saul changed his name to "Paul" to show Jesus had changed him from a murderer to a missionary.

Early in the trip, John-Mark left Paul and Barnabas. The work was too hard, so he went home to Jerusalem. But Barnabas and Paul continued sharing the gospel, no matter what happened to them. They led many people to Jesus and started churches in lots of cities. After the trip was over, they talked about going on another trip.

"I think John-Mark is ready this time," said Barnabas. "Let's give him a second chance."

"No way," said Paul. "He left us. If you want to take him, go ahead. But I'll pick someone else to go with me."

Barnabas was sad to leave Paul, but he believed John-Mark would serve God well if he just had another chance. Barnabas took John-Mark on a new trip, and Paul took Silas with him. Paul and Silas took three trips and started many new churches. Paul wrote letters to those churches, teaching them how to follow Jesus. He mentioned his helpers in every letter. He even mentioned John-Mark (sometimes called "Mark") in a few letters because John-Mark became a good helper to Paul and the other missionaries, just like Barnabas thought he would.

Barnabas gave Paul and John-Mark second chances, and they both became important leaders in the church.

Focus Verse

One of the believers was named Joseph. The apostles called him Barnabas, a name that means "one who encourages others."

ACTS 4:36, ERV

Talk About It

» How was Barnabas a special friend to Paul?

» Why did Barnabas give John-Mark a second chance?

» Why is it good to give someone a second chance?

LET'S PRAY

DEAR GOD, thank You for giving me so many chances to say I'm sorry for my sins. Help me to be a special friend to people who need another chance to do right. Amen.

Love All People

James 2

JAMES WAS ONE of Jesus' brothers. After Jesus came back to life, James believed that Jesus was the Son of God. James wanted followers of Jesus to treat all people with love and kindness the way that Jesus did. James wrote a letter to show Jesus' followers how to live with compassion.

James said, "Dear people, you believe in Jesus, our Lord and Savior, so don't treat some people better than others. What if a rich person comes to your meeting wearing nice clean clothes and a shiny gold ring. You treat him like an important person and say, 'You may sit here in this good seat.' At the same time a poor person comes in wearing dirty old, ragged clothes. You treat him like he's not important and say, 'Go stand over there,' or, 'You may sit on the floor by our feet.' This shows that you think some people are more important than others. But God chose the poor people in the world to be rich in faith. They become part of God's family when they believe in Jesus."

In his letter, James reminded people to do what Jesus said, "Love your neighbor as you love yourself." Then James added, "If you do this, you are doing what's right." James also told people if they showed mercy to others with love and forgiveness, then God would show mercy to them.

In his letter, James gave another example of how to treat others. He said, "What if someone comes to you and needs food or clothes? Then you say to that person, 'God is with you and will take care of you. I hope you stay warm and get enough to eat.' But if you don't give that person food or clothes, your words don't help them at all! Helping others by doing something shows that you have faith in Jesus."

James told the people, "It's good that you believe in God. It's good that you have faith in Jesus. But show me how much faith you have by helping others and doing good things for them."

James taught people how to treat each other with love.

193

Focus Verse

Listen, my dear brothers! God chose the poor in the world to be rich with faith. He chose them to receive the kingdom God promised to people who love Him.

JAMES 2:5, ICB

Talk About It

» Why did James write a letter to Jesus' followers?

» What commandment did James talk about?

» How can you show love to someone who has a need?

DEAR GOD, I know You love everyone the same. Help me to treat everyone with love the way You want me to. Amen.

A New World

Revelation 1; 21:1-5, 11-21

JOHN WAS ONE OF JESUS' twelve disciples. After Jesus went back to heaven, John and the other disciples traveled around the world, telling everyone about Jesus. Wherever Jesus' disciples went, more people began to believe in Jesus. Many leaders and rulers didn't like this, so they hurt the disciples or put them in prison. John was sent to an island in Greece, called Patmos, to keep him from telling people about Jesus.

One day, while John was praying, an angel gave him a vision of heaven. He heard a loud voice like a trumpet blast say to him, "Write in a book everything you see and send it to the churches."

John turned to see who was speaking to him. The man was wearing a long robe with a gold ribbon across His chest. His hair was as white as snow, and His eyes were like flames of fire. His feet were like glowing brass, and His voice was loud like an ocean. His face shone bright like the sun. John had to shield his eyes. He realized the man was Jesus, and he fell on his knees to worship.

Jesus put His hand on John and said, "Don't be afraid. I am the Living One. I died, but now I'm alive, and I will live forever."

In John's vision, an angel showed him a new heaven and a new earth. He saw the Holy City, where God's glory shone like bright jewels. The gates of the city were made from pearls and the streets were made of pure gold.

John heard a voice say, "God's home will be with His people. God will live with them. He will be their God, and they will be His people. He will wipe away every tear from their eyes. There won't be any more death or sadness or crying. No one will have pain. I am making everything new!"

John wrote about the vision God gave Him so everyone would know that someday God will make everything right and He will live with His people forever.

God loves us so much that He is preparing a beautiful place for us in heaven.

Focus Verse

He will wipe away every tear from
their eyes. There will be no more
death, sadness, crying, or pain.
All the old ways are gone.

REVELATION 21:4, ERV

Talk About It

» Why was John sent to Patmos?

» Who did John see in his vision?

» Why will heaven be wonderful?

LET'S PRAY

DEAR GOD, thank You that Jesus is coming
back someday. Thank you that I can live in
heaven with You forever. Amen.

How to become a believer in Jesus

God wants a relationship with you.

*For this is how God loved the world: He gave His one
and only Son, so that everyone who believes in Him
should not perish but have eternal life.*

JOHN 3:16, NLT

Sin separates us from God.

*For everyone has sinned;
we fall short of God's glorious standard.*

ROMANS 3:23, NLT

You cannot earn salvation.

*God saved you by His grace when you believed.
And you can't take credit for this; it is a gift from God.
Salvation is not a reward for the good things we have done,
so none of us can boast about it.*

EPHESIANS 2:8-9, NLT

Jesus died for your sins.

*God showed His great love for us by sending Christ
to die for us while we were still sinners.*

ROMANS 5:8, NLT

You can know that you are saved.

*If you openly declare that Jesus is Lord and believe in your
heart that God raised Him from the dead, you will be saved.*

ROMANS 10:9, NLT

Dear God,

I know I'm a sinner, and I can't be good
enough to earn my way to heaven.

I believe Jesus died on the cross
for my sins and rose again.
Please forgive me of my sins
and be the Lord of my life.
I love You.

In Jesus' name,
Amen.

About the Authors

Crystal Bowman is a bestselling, award-winning author of more than 100 books for children and families. She is the creator and co-author of *Our Daily Bread for Kids, M is for Manger,* and *I Love You to the Stars—When Grandma Forgets, Love Remembers.* She is also a conference speaker, freelance editor, and contributor to several

blogs. More than 3 million copies of her books have sold internationally, and her books have been translated into more than a dozen languages. She is a regular contributor to *Clubhouse Jr. Magazine,* and writes lyrics for children's piano music. She and her husband enjoy spending time with their grown children and eight huggable grandkids.

Sue Schlesman is an award-winning author, teacher, and church leader. In 2020, Sue won a Selah Award for her nonfiction book *Soulspeak: Praying Change into Unexpected Places.* Sue is a top-contributor to *Salem Web Network* radio ministry and *Crosswalk.com.* Sue has taught children of every age and sponsors children in poverty around the world. She loves traveling, reading, missions, art, and dessert. Sue has a BA in Creative Writing and a Masters in Theology and Culture. Sue is agented with Karen Neumair at Credo Communications.